10/

5/

D0759473

1975

A

4⁵⁰

OLD AGE IN EUROPEAN SOCIETY

OLD AGE
IN EUROPEAN SOCIETY

THE CASE OF FRANCE

PETER N. STEARNS

CROOM HELM   LONDON

Croom Helm Ltd.
2-10 St John's Road, London, SW11

ISBN 0-85664-307-6

Printed and bound in Great Britain by
REDWOOD BURN LIMITED
Trowbridge and Esher

CONTENTS

TABLES

ACKNOWLEDGMENTS

I would like to thank John Simon Guggenheim Memorial Foundation for the grant that supported the bulk of this research. I am grateful also to Carnegie-Mellon University which supported some of the necessary tabulations of data.

Dr Theodore Zeldin and Dr Patricia Branca both read portions of the manuscript and provided extremely useful advice. I am also grateful to Dr Andrew Achenbaum for his suggestions.

To the memory of Elizabeth Scott Stearns

PREFACE

Among the most anguishing problems modern industrial societies face
and will face increasingly is that of aging. The use of verb tenses
present and future is tragic; we should be able to say 'have faced' as
well. For the elderly have encountered special problems, as a segment
of the population, for centuries, yet with few exceptions they have
been ignored by the broader society. If they fell into categories of
'the poor' or 'the disabled' they might receive attention but not as
old people *per se*, even when society was increasingly refining its
concern for infants, children, adolescents, women, workers and a
host of other definable social groups. To be sure pension plans
developed as part of early benefit programs offered by governments
and some private organizations. They have been elaborated since in
welfare systems. For those without supplements they remain
inadequate, and the material problems of the aged will loom large
in the following pages. But the elderly themselves now indicate
that material concerns are outweighed by problems of personal
and societal adjustment. These have gained scant heed from public
authorities, not only the state but institutions such as labor unions.
They are vitally in need of study from various vantage-points, for
with understanding key difficulties may prove open to remedy.

Social scientific, as opposed to medical, attention to the elderly
is rather new. It was first developed by economists properly
concerned with the funding implications of a society in which a
growing minority will be retired, not only non-productive but
an active drain on public resources. And if initially the elderly
sector expanded mainly because birth rates shrank, since the
1930s it has grown rapidly on its own with rising adult longevity. The
aged are not just rivaling children as a non-producing sector, they
are gaining on them; yet it is hard to be as sympathetic toward
social expenses for a group whose proximate fate is death as for one
that can be trained to be future producers. So the economists'
calculations tend toward gloom, as they contemplate future pension
requirements, although the more perceptive grant possibilities of
changing definitions and functions for older people.

More recently sociologists have added their mite, and the
proliferation of institutes of gerontology, with a heavy social science

component, reflects belated public interest in the problems of aging and belated but growing sociological concern with the same. 'Here is an important gain, even if its best fruits remain to mature. For only a general social science approach, beyond a dollars and cents calculation, can offer new understanding of the aged, new solutions to their problems, hopefully, and new definitions of their social role.

Historians have made a still more tardy turn to any attention to the elderly. There was a false start. Simone de Beauvoir's book *The Coming of Age* received undue attention, despite the inadequacy of its research base and hosts of erroneous conclusions which in fact insulted the group for which the author expresses great sympathy. The author's renown played a role in the book's reception, but there was also a thirst for some broader perspective in time. Professional historians shunned the topic even after this. Unlike other social scientists they were offered no public funds to support research until very recently. This is in part the historians' fault, for they resolutely refuse to define their research in terms of current public problems, lest they be relevant and helpful. In this sense the present book, a pilot effort, is an attempt to apply history in new ways. It brings its topic into the present day. It suggests policy needs and possibly even policy solutions, thus bridging the gap between social history and sociology. Aspects of the modern history of aging are indeed surprisingly contemporary, for as a group the elderly have been the last to undergo clear effects from the modernization process. Indeed, as we study trends, we can see that they are in midstream, with a host of options open, whether for better or for worse.

We need histories of the elderly for various reasons, and not because historians, having ignored the subject before, can give themselves new interests by adding this to their arsenal. We need history because other academicians cannot keep their hands off it yet study it not and err in their facile generalizations. Sociological gerontology abounds with introductions concerning the declining place of old people in modern society, displaced from the patriarchal eminence of the respectful village. This correctly demonstrates the need for historical perspective, a groping for some sense of where the modern elderly fit in a time scheme. But it is an unexamined hypothesis, designed mainly to create a lachrymose atmosphere and gaining credence by repetition alone. Further, no stages within modern society's development have been examined. With industrialization and urbanization the old people are an alienated, isolated lump, incapable of reaction. In fact we will see various shadings within the modern rubric and responses adding up to trends which must be grasped if the elderly themselves are to be understood. So we have vital scholarly reasons for treating the elderly through an innovative historical approach.

But we do not stop with academese. A study of the elderly cannot help but raise social concern. This is not new to history, of course. Workers, women and other groups have gained sound historical study designed to elicit sympathy for their present lot as well. This study differs in seizing on a topic that has not clearly been politicized: the left cannot claim much more than the right, which as we will see raises real problems for old people even if it helps the historian avoid distracting political polemic. It differs in directly taking the subject to the present, rather than using nineteenth-century analogies (how bad things were in the 1830s) to convey what is intended to be a contemporary message (how bad things still are since the system is the same). If we are concerned about current trends let us trace them into their currency. The study differs substantially from work on other oppressed elements in taking a subject for which few vocal movements exist. The elderly have not developed their equivalent of a labor movement or feminism to date. They need all the spokesmen, all the vantage-points, they can get.

As an attempt to add history to the disciplines that cast light on the situation of old people we must admit to a key problem. What follows is not informed with any definite sense of what the elderly should do with their lives. Indeed it seems clear that formulas are to be shunned, as the elderly vary more by social class and individual temperament than any other definable segment of society. So far the most successful overall approach to aging seems to be to act young, with suitable precautions and modifications. As the following pages repeatedly suggest, hoary admonitions to 'act your age' are inappropriate and damaging. This is the problem. Without casting aside all past wisdom on the topic, we do venture to editorialize, and critically, about much of it. Yet we do not mean thereby to embrace the newer youth culture wholeheartedly; this will hopefully prove a way-station to a genuine but new definition of old age appropriate to the stage of life itself. We intend to refine the problem, indicate some approaches that have been counterproductive, and trace the origins and depth of the youth tactic that is now touted as the wave of the future. Aspects of all these judgments, particularly those suggesting what should not be done, involve a set of values, beginning with the premiss that the elderly can and should be active, participant members of their society, for their own well-being if nothing else. But I cannot presume to define exactly what activities are best, what forms participation should take. I believe that objective historical study can assist individual older people and policy-makers alike to understand the framework within which decisions have to be made.

For above all the following essays are offered with the firm conviction that the elderly and those that deal with them have long been trapped by history, almost unconsciously. While recent developments, largely initiated by older people themselves, have loosened the trap, it can be fully released only as history itself is explored. Historical study brings two fundamental messages: first, an understanding of the incredibly deep and varied roots of a culture that has denigrated the elderly in the eyes of those who take them in charge and, worse, in their own eyes. Second, more hopefully, an indication of methods by which a new culture can be developed, not just by heroes of gerontology – Michelangelo, Victor Hugo – but by the run-of-the-mill older person, which, statistically, almost all of us will end up being for a time. We deal of necessity with groups – the aged in general, women, distinct social classes – because we are trying to grasp the common situations of the past and their heritage to the present. But aging is an individual matter, and there is no sign that sweeping policies can remove the necessity for self-understanding as one enters, willy-nilly, the final phase, which we now bedeck with euphemisms of senior citizenry or 'the third age.' I would like to believe that historical consciousness can aid this self-understanding, for people for whom the past has unusual reality.

As historians begin to jump onto the gerontological bandwagon we can expect a spate of precise studies of the elderly in particular areas and limited time periods, all done with great sophistication, often embellished with detailed statistics. This book constitutes a more general effort to combine types of sources – cultural materials, statistics, a few local samplings – but it may not please those who feel we should begin with cautious empirical building blocks before we venture an architectural scheme or total edifice. We wish to sketch the edifice, by touching on a variety of types of problems over a long timespan. One could, for example, focus on census and related materials alone to show where the elderly have lived, with whom, to what age, by variables such as class, sex, and region and hopefully with the possibility of developing a sense of evolution over time. We offer elements of such a study but much remains to be done. The concern is for a more general portrayal of the historical background to contemporary aging, a background which so intimately merges with the present that neither can be understood without the other.

Inevitably, in this process, questions must be raised that are not yet fully answered. Let me mention two leading ones, by way of indicating the major problem areas involved. We must refer constantly to the issue sociologists evoke, that of preindustrial versus industrial conditions and mentalities. New evidence is offered on the subject and my own judgment, that the preindustrial heritage was wanting, is tossed in as well. But the following essays do not involve the detailed study really needed; we cannot pretend to be sure what the normal status of key groups of older persons in preindustrial society was, yet this is a question that must somehow be answered. My impulse, relying on scattered evidence and on secondary studies that have not focused on the elderly *per se* (such as witchcraft materials which deal with old women not as such, but simply because they produce a disproportionate number of accused witches[2]) is to urge avoidance of the 'golden age' *mythos* that has surrounded every major subject in social history. Workers were better off back then, women have been ruined by industrialization; old people bid fair to join this parade. I think we should study this rather than guess, and if a debate is already launched through the common impression (not shared by older people[3]) that things were better 'then,' then I must admit to a desire to debunk. And this not only because the impression at the least oversimplifies the preindustrial past — this much can be proved — but because, as with all the golden age approaches, it risks making its modern subjects seem like helpless pawns, even idiots, as they let themselves be acted upon. With the aged, I think there are two alternate possibilities that fit the facts better, and we must explore which is most probable. Possibility 1: industrialization, a complex phenomenon, involved initial deterioration (which does not impute classic qualities to the precedent society), but then subsequent improvement as the elderly learned to react rather than be acted upon. This approach involves a multi-level analysis, level a, down to level b followed by level c higher than either of the previous two, which is much more likely than the view that sees industrial society as a homogeneity. Possibility 2: changes in industrial society (for these will be documented in what follows) but from the first substantial progress over preindustrial conditions, which were varied but on average foul. Again, complete answers depend on further study of the preindustrial setting, which is eminently feasible.

The second unresolved problem concerns what old people did, until very recently at least, in retirement. We can trace what people were told to do in retirement, a definitely evolving pattern of advice. We can tell when people retired, in general. We can tell where retirees live and with whom. We know how many were institutionalized and what institutional policies were, though this turns out to be surprisingly unimportant, for good reason, as institutionalization has not played a great role in the lives of the elderly. But we have only the haziest notions of what old people did, what their functions, prestige and self-esteem were, after retirement. It remains widely assumed that agricultural people continue at least part-time work as they age; census-takers thus still list them as heads of family, if male. But this may be merely an updating of the part of the old golden age theory that equates rural life with the good life. The predominant urban situation, save as tapped by very recent polls, has a vaguer but negative mythology, with the elderly as possible baby-sitters but little else.[4] We can improve upon this but possibly never resolve the historical issues involved, because the elderly did not leave relevant sources and nobody bothered to study their lot in other than material and statistical terms. Thus this is a vital topic, perhaps more important than any other in understanding the problems of aging in our society, and one must speculate even if on the basis of scattered, often indirect evidence to suggest trends and conclusions. Of all the silent groups yet uncovered by historians dealing with history 'from the bottom up,' the elderly as a group (leaving aside the usually bitter old *literati* beloved in the de Beauvoir approach to the subject) remain the most inarticulate. This silence may be remedied, as it has been in the study of groups like slaves, once concentrated attention is directed to the elderly, but for the moment the gaps in sources leave questions but half answered.

Organizationally, in part because of the novelty of the subject, what follows falls between essay collection and narrative monograph. Periodization of the history of aging is still not defined. This is not a neat 'elderly in the early industrial period,' 'elderly at the turn of the century' approach, for we don't know enough yet for this step-by-step structure. It may prove not to be needed anyway, save for purposes of broadening understanding of a period, when what was being done to and by the elderly could embellish knowledge of the nature of a society in a vital and novel manner.

Instead, the following is a series of thematic essays, but with a crucial linkage. The main theme involves a dominant culture, the extent the elderly and key groups who dealt with them were and still are ensnared therein, and the nature of departures therefrom. Individual chapters trace variants on this theme: doctors are used as an example of the interaction between culture and a group dealing with the elderly, though politicians or the directors of homes for the aged could similarly be traced; so, as we will indicate, could younger adults in a family dealing with an older relative. Key groups are studied with an eye to distinct patterns of modernization, which involves particular attention to the working class and the middle class as those exposed to the leading edge of change, though the agricultural sector is not entirely ignored. Women are treated separately, as their aging process involves distinctive elements, but as these are mainly exacerbations of general problems this is handled more briefly. The sum of these segments, each of which can be examined separately, indicates, I believe, the kinds of topics that must be treated historically for any real understanding of the elderly not only by historians but by other scholars (doctors as well as social scientists) and by the elderly themselves and those who deal with them. The subject is too vital for the usual game of historians simply writing to other historians.

Partly for this reason, in the desire not to burden readers with too many historical conventions, partly because the book does follow a path not yet blazed, a few other technical liberties need mention. Footnoting is normally elaborate, and can be ignored or not as the reader wishes; but there is no general bibliography given the fact that the interested reader can follow references in the notes themselves and given the lack as yet of a body of literature on the subject to which a general reader can refer. (Literally one article by a professional historian exists on any aspect of the history of aging as of the present writing.[5]) Elaborate definitions of social class are not attempted. They can be found elsewhere[6] and for the elderly we lack information for the often tedious effort to say where, for example, middle class ends and workers begin. Chronology ranges freely in each essay, from the background to the modern era, defined simply and conventionally by the advent of significant industrialization-urbanization, to evolution within the modern era itself. For most topics a break or near-break is suggested for the last three or four decades, as the elderly began to make the turn to innovation.

Finally, by way of preliminaries, we focus on France as a logical starting point for two reasons. First France, along with Sweden, earliest had the highest proportion of elderly in the population, a function in the French case mainly of the rapidly declining birth rate. Theoretically this might put special strain on institutions, families, even individuals, so that problems later to be encountered elsewhere, as over ten percent of the population fell into the over-65 age category for the first time in history, were first raised in France. As we will indicate, there is almost no evidence of direct impact, as only the census-takers noted the phenomenon until after World War Two, save for a possible, largely unconscious negative effect: that the presence of unusually large numbers of elderly made certain groups particularly youth-conscious, lest they be swamped by the old. France was selected as a starting point, second, because of the high probability that a traditional culture toward the elderly antedated the modern phenomenon of aging, a culture durably respectful and deferential, as opposed to the brash youth worship of, say, the United States. Here, only comparative study can indicate how good a paradigm France is for a certain kind of approach to and by the elderly and how great a contrast exists between it and other kinds of societies. A few suggestions are ventured in several of the following chapters but a full, imaginative comparison remains desirable. For the moment, in helping to open a new subject, some limitation of the cultural-institutional variable was essential — hence the primary focus on a single country.

And so, for specific introduction, a few concrete facts about the elderly population in France, for reference in the substantive chapters that follow. For French history buffs, let me confess that while I firmly believe that old age must be added to the topics considered standard in the development of modern French society, we find few familiar landmarks. The vaunted French proclivity for old politicians in times of crisis (Clemenceau, Pétain, de Gaulle) does not carry over into general attitudes toward aging, and French commentaries on old age rightly cite such men as exceptions that prove no rule. Syndicalism plays a mild role in working-class outlook toward preparing for aging, but it is not decisive; a broader culture is in force here. The gradual character of French urbanization may leave a distinctive mark, as the elderly long turn to the countryside. But French individualism, French slowness in developing welfare programs including pensions, French combativeness — such oft-cited characteristics are either inaccurate, as largely holds true for pension development, or if applicable to other features of modern French life not discernibly useful in studying the aging process. So first a brief set of factual guidelines for a new field that will deserve integration into broader strands of French history, even if our present concern is primarily to use France as a case study of culture and behavior that may be generalizable beyond national boundaries, as tradition plus the particular debilities of old age encountered modernization.[7]

In 1900 8.2 percent of the French population was over 65. Only Sweden exceeded this, at 8.3 percent. Belgium, at 6.2 percent, Holland at 6.0 percent, England-Wales at 4.7 percent and the United States at 4.0 percent were far more typical of industrial countries. France did not enjoy a favorable adult life expectancy. At age 50 a French male could expect 19.5 more years of life, an Englishman or Welshman 20.3 and a Swede 22.6. France's gerontological lead thus stemmed exclusively from the extraordinarily low birth rate, which automatically increased the percentage of elderly in the population. Longevity did improve in France — by 1920 it stood at 20.7 years for a fifty-year-old male; but only since World War Two has it exceeded rates in other industrial countries. 1950 marked the year when, at 22.3, it beat England and Wales (at 22.2). In 1967 male life expectancy at 50 was 23.3 in France, compared to Sweden's 25.8, but England and Wales' 22.7 and Belgium's 23.2. Older people in France experienced a major break in life experience, which life expectancy both reflected and promoted, in the 1930s and 1940s. The break was sharper than that in most other industrial nations, though similar in basic trend.

In France as in other countries older people were least likely to die if married. Bachelors and spinsters had the lowest life expectancy. But widows did quite well, normally outliving spinsters and sometimes even married women. Widowers, on the other hand, invariably had less chance than married men and sometimes less chance than elderly bachelors. Here is a differential that necessitates exploration in a subsequent chapter, for we must try to explain why men fare worse in old age, and increasingly worse with modernization, than women on a comparative basis. In 1963 a bachelor was 9 percent more likely to die in a given year, after 60 years of age, than a widower (after 70 it mattered less, at 0.2 percent). A married man was 31 percent less likely to die, and after 70, 24 percent, than a widower. But the durable female demonstrated the same death rates whether spinster or widow. If married she graciously died 17 percent less often than her stubborn or bereaved sisters, in the ages 60-69, 24 percent less often annually after age 70.[8]

France thus has long had an exceptionally large elderly population, but until recently this resulted from no particularly benign treatment; indeed the phenomenon was neither studied nor provided for. Here is a certain uniqueness, but France was to a substantial extent merely preceding other countries in gerontological neglect; hence the validity of exploring its history. Other patterns, such as sex differentials, are completely typical, and can be studied and explained as paradigms. France could not rival claims from the Caucasus or the Andes as to the extremes of longevity. But as early as 1856, in the mountains of Paris, 17 people were centenarians; in France overall, 113. The old existed, quite apart from the extreme accomplishment of a century's span. Their situation and behavior evolved, which is only saying that they had a history, which in turn is only saying that they were human beings.

One final matter, applicable to France or any other country: what constitutes old age? Medical definitions, as we will see, have evolved from rather rigid, classical terminology in which men were old at 65, women at 50 (exact ages varied, but the principle was clear) to more flexible, cuter phrases such as 'one is as old as one's arteries.' Definitions do vary by individual. Retirement ages reflect this, falling into no neat pattern: out at 60 or 65 is at best a median (and only for men; women, aging in many respects later than men, retire earlier). Definitions certainly differ by class; in 1900 there were those, perhaps a majority at least in the cities, who believed they were or would be old at 45. So the question really combines attitude and biology, and we must leave it as a question, to be answered variably depending on the subject. As a practical matter, particularly when statistics were involved, our research generally began with age 55, a bit later than some cultural perceptions of aging but anticipating most distinctive behavior (in work, family structure, sex, and medical treatment) associated with biological aging. The perceptions, however, we pick up as they were stated, even when this involves tracing deterioration of hearing to age 30 or working-class belief that after 40 everything was downhill or the persistent conviction on the part of many women and those dealing with women that everything is lost with menopause. For in final analysis we have to let aging begin when people think it begins. This involves arteries, and an immense amount of history.

Notes

1. Social science works on aging abound. Leo Simmons, *Old Age in Pre-Industrial Societies* (New Haven, 1948), presents a classic conventional view. Other works with some historical frame of reference include Matilda W. Riley *et al., Aging and Society* (2v. New York, 1968-72); Ethel Shanas *et al., Old People in Three Industrial Societies* (New York, 1968); Bernice L. Neugarten (ed.), *Middle Age and Aging* (Chicago, 1960); and S.N. Eisenstadt, *From Generation to Generation* (Chicago, 1956). French work has been characteristically less active and more derivative; see Centre international de gérontologie sociale, *Loisirs et 3e Age* (Paris, 1972) and Paul Paillat, *Sociologie de la vieillesse* (Paris, 1963).
2. Keith Thomas, *Witchcraft in English Society* (London, 1963), and various articles.
3. Caisse nationale de retraite des ouvriers du bâtiment et travaux publics, *Réalités du troisième age: Enquête sur les ouvriers retraités du bâtiment et des travaux publics* (Paris, 1969), p.68 and *passim.*
4. Michael Anderson, *Family Structure in Nineteenth Century Lancashire* (Cambridge, 1973).
5. Andrew Achenbaum, 'The Obsolescence of Old Age in America,' *Journal of Social History* (1974), pp.48-62.
6. Peter N. Stearns, *European Society in Upheaval* (New York, 1973), *passim.*
7. In the late eighteenth century a twenty-year-old Frenchman had a 36 percent chance of reaching old age; only 8 percent of all people 60-70 years of age died annually. Hence an estimate, inherently approximate, yields the conclusion that 13 percent of the adult population over twenty was over 60 years of age, and 2 percent over 70. The old were not distinctively scarce, the very young, half of them about to die, simply overabundant, which has thrown off countless calculations of the position of the elderly. Fernand Boverrt, *Le Vieillissement de la population* (Paris, 1946).
8. *Statistique de la France, Mouvement de la Population,* 1956ff; see also census materials, which include international comparisons of age category percentages. The figures here are *per capita within* each group; on an absolute basis a higher percentage of married women die, simply because there are more of them.

1 THE EVOLUTION OF TRADITIONAL CULTURE TOWARD AGING

Old age is an age-old problem, and a distinct culture has surrounded it for centuries. Western civilization may have taken an unusually nasty attitude toward the old, but as this is not a cross-cultural comparison we can only suggest this, not elaborate upon it. Simone de Beauvoir's book, in its strongest section, dramatically demonstrates the hostility with which old age was viewed by top intellectuals, Seneca and the like, from ancient times onward. Popular culture reflected similar values: old age was a horror and old people a great nuisance. Far from the traditional veneration for old age which one might expect to find in France — which I had expected to pursue, in fact, in launching this study — one finds almost unmitigated disdain. This disdain persisted well into the contemporary era, among those who dealt with older people, among old people themselves most tragically, and among those who contemplated growing old.

This is why we begin with culture — not the great writers, but those who purported to address themselves to old people, who were popularizers and mirrors of widespread societal attitudes. Obviously there is danger in dealing with 'culture' in this sense. The manuals and articles utilized were not widely read; only one, in the nineteenth century, went through more than three editions. But they did proliferate, which suggests some growth in readership and social concern. What is important, however, is not their direct impact so much as their correspondence with more elusive general attitudes. This was a widespread set of values, whatever their precise connections, and the values failed to sustain the old in either pre-modern or modern society.

Two preliminaries, however, to the ultimate connection between published material and popular opinion, which posits that from intellectual to villager, ancient attitudes persisted into recent times. Old people were not new — in other words, traditional wisdom had not been formed in a vacuum or only at the upper-class level. And, obviously, traditional veneration of the elderly (which is predicated in part on their presumed rarity) is largely mythical. Which latter means in turn, to anticipate a bit, that our problems in dealing with old people go far deeper than the evils of capitalism or the hedonism of modern youth; they lie deep in our cultural heritage and it will require heroic efforts, led by the contemporary elderly themselves, to undo the web.

There is a basic demographic confusion which pops up in the most surprising scholarly writing. 'At the beginning of the century the expectation of life of women in our countries was about 45. At present it is an average 75 or more. Thirty years longer to live.'[1] We have already seen in the French case that the implication that few people lived to what we would call old age in preindustrial times is untrue. Life expectancy has increased because, primarily, of the massive decline in infant mortality. If an ordinary person survived age two (before which his or her chances of dying were 50 percent) the prospect of living into the fifties, at least, was pretty good. Yet we have a pervasive impression that the only old people in Western society were the rich and unusual: 'The small group of people who lived into old age. . .was generally composed of the aristocracy or the wealthy middle class.'[2] Simone de Beauvoir has similarly stated that the old barely existed until the late eighteenth century (which makes her elaborate tracing of a culture of old age a bit futuristic) and that then their gradual appearance was purely an upper-class phenomenon.[3] The fact is, as we have seen, that among adults in a preindustrial village (where admittedly half the population was by definition normally under two) a good 6-8 percent were 'elderly', using this term loosely as being over 55. The percentage of elderly actually decreased in the late eighteenth century and into the nineteenth, because of the larger number of surviving children, though longevity seems to have improved a slight bit. But in late eighteenth-century France a statistical projection, admittedly tentative, indicated that only 34 percent of the population between 20 and 39 would die before reaching 40, and that on attaining adulthood one had a 36 percent chance of reaching the general area of old age (55-60 years of age). The old were definite fixtures in a preindustrial setting, and often annoying ones.

For these figures are not tossed about simply to confound a demographic confusion, though it would be delightful if otherwise intelligent people would stop using terms like 'scarcity value' to distort the situation of the preindustrial elderly. The point is that the elderly were about, at all levels of society, and in considerable numbers. Attainment of one's sixties, while impressive, was hardly rare enough to call forth outpourings of awe. And all groups in society, not just the upper classes, had to develop attitudes and behavior patterns toward the elderly, which is what this section is all about. Traditionalism was not developed in a vacuum.

This relates to the second preliminary, already mentioned because it is so vital in interpreting the evolution of the elderly. Veneration of the old — esteem for the white-bearded patriarch or the sage grandmother dispensing wisdom from her rocking chair — could not develop from sheer rareness. Yet the social science literature on aging depends heavily on the notion that with modernization the number of old people increases and their worth is diminished among other things because they are so common.[4] Numbers increase, to be sure, but percentages go down in the intermediate period of demographic revolution and rise only in the later nineteenth century after capitalism's callous ways are well established. But the literature goes on with more persuasive arguments, particularly with regard to the twentieth century. Improved health is granted, but this merely allows more people to reach old age and find it disappointing. Material standards have risen, but not so rapidly as those of other groups in the population. Above all, in a culture that measures worth by productivity and does not depend on experience for wisdom, the role the elderly play has shrunk. Family decay leaves them isolated, where once they ruled the clan. Popular assumption echoes this theme of declension; public opinion polls in France as late as the 1940s revealed that a majority believed that longevity itself had declined in modern times.[5] Modernization and deterioration seem inextricably intertwined for the elderly.

This is not a logical connection. We can grant immense problems for the elderly at the present time, but we do not have to assume that their lot has ever been strikingly good in Western society. History is wrapped up in the difficulties of old people, but because of traditional mistreatment more than modern innovations.

Yet the few cultural historians who have touched on the subject of aging have tried to confirm the deterioration motif. A recent article on American culture picks up the point nicely. Middle-class magazines portrayed the elderly with great sympathy and appreciation until the later nineteenth century, when the stress began to switch to the miseries and inutility of old age.[6] The venerable patriarch, still smithying under the spreading tree, became a social drone. There may be some truth in this, but two initial caveats: first, it does not explain the outburst of American 'it's fun to be old' literature which appeared in the 1920s, of which more later. And second, it does not compare neatly with a more traditional society such as France, where one might expect veneration of old age to continue for a longer period.

Simone de Beauvoir's work presents a slight variant on the same theme. She also notes deterioration in the view of the elderly by the end of the nineteenth century, but believes that briefly, in French culture, there was a pride in age, when authors like Victor Hugo (if only for self-justification, as they lived in health into their eighties) gloried the old and found virtue in age. This outlook was to end with the youth-oriented twentieth century, so that whatever twists are taken with pre- and early-nineteenth-century material, we return inexorably to the theme of deterioration.

This approach is basically incorrect, for the old have consistently been treated unkindly in Western culture with exceptions, which can include Hugo, Longfellow, but also Cicero, to be found proving the rule. And here, before launching on nineteenth-century attitudes more precisely, which largely mirrored traditional themes for the simple reason that these were not rethought, let us dip into probable pre-modern attitudes, which is why we venture an initial cultural chapter in a social history of the elderly in the first place.

Picture the aging villager. We know he/she was not rare. Extraordinary individuals may have maintained great power, if they preserved their health and/or could claim access to unusual wisdom, not excluding magical powers or more prosaic talents such as midwifery (which in countries like England and France involved however only appointment by the local pastor and the fact of having had children oneself).[7] The old might preserve a place. But the more typical situation involved such mundane matters as the probable loss of teeth by age 45. This meant that someone, typically the youngest daughter who would not marry among other things because of a decade or more of care of an aging parent, had to chop up food and spoon it down the elderly gullet. False teeth became a common purchase among the lower classes only after 1850. The old might cling to property ownership, long after they were judged incapable of making sensible decisions about its use or actually working the fields. We can jump to the end of the nineteenth century when a French peasant expressed a typical attitude. Writing of his father's demise he remarked only: 'When in 1891 after the death of my father, I became free to act as I wanted. . .'[8] So many peasants did retire, but in so doing they commonly had to protect themselves carefully against the ambitions of their children; this was a major area of peasant law, for the aging parent who did not bind his property to support him as he grew too weak to till the land often found himself near starvation. Hence the careful legal provisions turning over cottages and produce to the elderly as they bequeathed the main property to the more capable successor generation.[9] The old were a nuisance. The commonplaces that prevailed about aging were largely pessimistic. Older widows, as we will see, were an object of special suspicions, not only in bouts of witchcraft mania but in normal times; an attempt at remarriage was regarded as inappropriate, often attended by rowdy charivari, while at the same time the widow, having fulfilled her function of bearing children and yet incapable of caring for property, was regarded as a village misfit. This is why a traditional society such as France long maintained a legacy of suspicion about aging which has yielded only in the past half-century, and then slowly and incompletely, to new attitudes. It was in fact newer, more youth-oriented cultures such as that of the United States (and perhaps transformed cultures as in the Soviet Union) that proved more flexible in their thinking about what old age is or might be.

Yet one other point about preindustrial culture in France and elsewhere. If the old were not statistically rare, few people could sensibly contemplate growing old. Death was omnipresent in the village. Infants died at rates of 50 percent or more; summer, the worst period in terms of infection and malnutrition (note the contrast with the modern cycle, when old people are most likely to die in winter) was a time of death. A mid-nineteenth-century Sicilian peasant saw eight of his playmates die when he was six, and only about half of the infants born at his age had even survived to six. Childhood was a time of fear, and few people could think of longevity. In a large Italian village a funeral occurred every three days, and more often during the summer. Death had to be accepted as normal, but it was mourned and remembered − and fought, with peasant remedies. For the young adult, the expectation that half one's children would die simply enhanced the disinterest, the disbelief, in aging.[10]

Peasant culture thus provided a durable basis for concentration on the now. Being elderly meant being an economic drain and was unrealistically unexpected, because of the pervasiveness of death at other age levels. This is the final element of the preindustrial outlook that would at once coincide with more formal culture and persist, as in the new urban working class, literally to the present day.

We turn now to the written word, with a pledge to return to evidence of correspondence between the published word and popular attitudes. The written image was, as already noted, not new; it corresponded to popular attitudes but also to most classical dictums about old age. What was new, in nineteenth-century France, was the number of pamphlets and articles on the subject, part of the general expansion of publishing more than of any recognition that old age posed novel problems or that the old were increasing in numbers. Census-takers noted the increased proportion of older people in the later nineteenth century, but who reads censuses? and they misconstrued the cause to boot, claiming better health rather than the simple effect of declining birth rates. The first public discussion of the social problems of aging came only after World War Two, when France was feeling low; here it was recognised that a sluggish birth rate and, now, rising longevity would produce a less vibrant population, which combined correct demographic facts with the traditional view of the old as useless which really must serve as our main theme.[11]

The increased writing on aging in the nineteenth century had two specific sources. First, the rise of science and medicine, which will be detailed more fully in the next chapter. Buffon and others gave new scientific cachet to the investigation of centenarians,[12] with the basic theme that most people do not manage to live out their normal lifespan.[13] More specific of course was the concern of doctors. Discussions of menopause, for example, began in the eighteenth century and increased steadily, and continue to the present. Doctors accounted for many of the pamphlets and books designed to tell people how to live a long life and what, if anything, to do with it. Some of their works won modest popularity, for the second source of the new materials on aging was the fact of a growing number of articulate older people, particularly in the middle classes, who wanted advice about this phenomenon, from presumed experts, just as they sought advice on child-rearing and marriage. At an admittedly lower level, then, we have the characteristic groping for guidance, produced by a larger group of people who were aware that they would become old or were indeed old, and wanted some control over their lot: a middle-class characteristic above all. Hence a book like Noirot's *L'Art de Vivre Longtemps,* published in 1868, went through eight editions. *La Verte Vieillesse,* written by a Lyons doctor in 1920, was widely read. In combination, the popularized works on aging by doctors, self-appointed experts, plus a few more conventional productions by old men themselves, eager to tell the whole world how they'd done it,[14] account for a substantial body of modern literature. All of this made the culture of aging more accessible than ever before.

And, in terms of the permeation of culture, the literature can be tested by its currency in general periodicals and, by the twentieth century, through direct statements by old people and their organizations. It had currency, even when its products were not

directly read. There are traces of rebellion against it, but these have been
arduous and remain incomplete partly because the culture is so persuasive,
and by no means entirely incorrect in its description of old age. But
it represents a self-fulfilling picture, which is why we must begin with it
and ultimately deplore it.

Despite a new audience and more scientific authors, the outlook
toward old age changed little from the eighteenth century to the
interwar period. Gloom prevailed even as Victor Hugo hailed his
undeniably persistent virility. Balzac portrayed the miseries of
retirement; Lamennais, Péguy and many others talked of age as a foul
infirmity. One cannot look to literature for a pervasive new current of
optimism. The classics were endlessly repeated, admittedly with some
internal contradiction as old age had not been a subject of antique
unanimity. One could be mildly optimistic with Cicero, deeply
aggrieved with Juvenel or Seneca. This classical framework was not
altered because old age, while commanding some new attention, was
not held to be important enough to merit serious new thought. The
one partial exception to this statement, clinical pathology, ironically
confirmed the classical pessimism. The ongoing culture of aging left
the increasing numbers of people who were old bereft of much
constructive advice about what they could do with the remainder of
their lives.

The repetition of past wisdom was endless. Cicero and Seneca are
perhaps less surprising than half-baked medical references to the cures
and definitions of Hippocrates and Galen. Lacassagne, the Lyons
doctor who made a good thing out of this 1920 manual, invoked
not only these classics but also Montaigne (who had aged loudly but
gracelessly) and Pascal. And one manual fed on another; Reveillé-
Parise, who produced an uncomfortable amalgam of medical and
conventional wisdom at mid-century, was constantly cited.[15]

From the classics one learned that old age began at fifty-five to
sixty (forty-five to fifty for women). This conventional wisdom,
derived from the age ladder of Hippocrates, was endlessly repeated.
According to Hippocrates, a springtime of old age might be defined
up to 70; a green old age from 70 to 75; 'real' old age, 75 to 80;
ultimate, 80-90 and caducity, 90 onward — by which time death was
both certain and welcome.[16] Reveillé-Parise, in a slightly clinical
variant in which he had to stress physical decay, put the green period
from 55 to 65, admitting only that it might extend longer in individual
cases; in this period, physical decline might be compensated by
intellectual faculties that could be at their height even though, the

clinician returning, the brain had become smaller and was receiving less blood.[17] The figures themselves may seem unsurprising, since they correspond roughly with our own notions of the onset of old age, save in the special case of women. What must be stressed however, is that once old age occurred, whatever the labels attached to its various stages, it was not seriously distinguished from senility. As Reveillé-Parise's modifications of the classical scale suggest, if a fertile period of old age was identified it involved pushing back the beginning of aging itself into what we would call later middle age.

This had a more dramatic and more obviously inaccurate corollary. Since old age could be defined so neatly, its arrival was believed to be quite sudden. Reveillé-Parise paints a picture of mature, robust health and appearance all at once giving way to the symptoms of age; hair grayed and fell out (sometimes a simultaneity was suggested that could best be explained by a change in color as the hair left the head and drifted to the floor); teeth fell out; organs deteriorated; wrinkles came, and so on. The pathologists correctly noted that the actual deterioration of organs was gradual, but they did not dispel the idea of a sudden change — most severe, of course, for women with the onset of menopause. The view survives, in the French term 'coup de vieux,' 'the blow of age.' Cosmeticians advise on how to conquer the *coup,* and even some doctors continue to stress that few people avoid it (though downplaying its brutality, in comparison with their nineteenth-century counterparts).[18] The 'coup de vieux' concept makes a stark contrast between normal adulthood and age, to the inevitable disadvantage of the latter. It emphasizes, again repeating classical wisdom, the irrevocability of a feeble old age.

To be sure, one could prepare for the last stage of life, and somewhat contradictorily, given the desire to define specific stages of aging, the classical legacy was more benign when it came to the question of how to reach old age in the first place. Cicero's wisdom was endlessly repeated, for again there was little new thinking, but with specified exceptions discussed below it was normally sound enough. Moderation was the key. The manuals argued about how much heredity played a role. It was generally agreed that short people, and thin people, had the best chance. Obesity was bad. Thick feet promised an early old age, as did a slow pulse. Noirot, the most popular of the manualists, argued against too much brain work; others were less sure. 'The immoderate exercise of the intellectual facilities can only tire the brain and exhaust that organ; intellectual work pushes back the limits of life.'[19] Most were convinced however that precocity was doomed to early demise. Athletes, also, were given low marks, because they spent themselves too early. But these factors of heredity or identifiability largely revolved around the moderation theme. Prepare for old age early, certainly by thirty-five or so. 'The wisdom of young men is the wealth or well-being of mature men, and health itself for old men.' Limit the passions, including sexual appetites. Exercise regularly but moderately — hard breathing should be avoided as 'the first sign of fatigue of the heart.'[20] Keep the eating down, particularly of meats, and obviously be moderate with wine. Get good air, and breath deeply (though presumably not too hard).[21] Maintain active interests but get lots of sleep; artists died young because of their irregular nocturnal habits. This same current of advice, though sensible enough in itself, produced a constant temptation to regard old age as a sickness, which could be prepared for only by the greatest prudence. Most medical manuals explicitly discounted the old-age-sickness equation and then proceeded to argue on its base.[22] Hence travel, for example, was bad. Reveillé-Parise noted: 'Old people are like old furniture; they last only so long as they stay put.' But there were warnings against vegetating, and the manuals uniformly opposed the idea of complete retirement.[23] The old had to feel useful and maintained 'an absolute need for an occupation, a task.'[24] Prudence could even conquer unfavorable heredity, so long as one did not wait until the onset of old age itself. Sobriety, nothing in excess — these were the keys to the kingdom.[25]

Recommendations changed almost not at all well into the twentieth century. Lacassagne, in 1920, added the desirability of regular medical visits to the list of virtues and an interest in 'scientific advances' to the contemplations available to the old, but little else had been altered. Thus the image of old age itself changed not at all; it might be slightly delayed by moderation, but this idea itself was not new. The preservation of the classical canons, even if sound, raised important problems for actual behavior in an urbanizing society, both for the old and for those contemplating the prospect of aging. Modernization brought rising material expectations that could easily conflict with the counsels of moderation. Manuals noted, for example, the contradiction between growing meat consumption and the proper preparation for old age. There resulted an interesting debate over the relationship between aging and modern times, which is significant particularly in its implicit contradiction with what modern people, prior to old age at least, were interested in doing with their rising wealth and their hedonism.

Beginning in the nineteenth century, there were many who began to believe that with modern ways longevity had deteriorated. As early as 1842 it was claimed that the modern life-style was 'richer in worries and frustrations than in happiness,' which was why man 'as now constituted' could not live to the Biblical term of 200 years.[26] Elie Metchnikoff, arguing for greater medical efforts to achieve man's natural life span, accepted Biblical claims as late as 1903; hence modern man did not live as long as his progenitors. The standard geriatric treatise published a few years later accepted the same opinion, noting that modern people hastened their own demise.[27] An advocate of 'hippocratic' medicine repeated this in 1940, for the traditional, almost mercantilistic belief that the body had a set amount of energy readily lent itself to the idea of increased modern depradations due to the new pace of life.[28] A more generalized variant on this argument was that average lifespan had improved, thanks to medical advance, but the number of people surviving to advanced age had declined. More popular opinion certainly accepted the idea. The *Gazette de Médicine* in 1861 listed the departments having the largest number of centenarians, noting with approval that most were rural but adding, with genuine astonishment: 'One is amazed to see the Seine included.' A woman's magazine admitted that many people used to look old at thirty but added, with the facile lack of consistency so common in discussing aging, that the modern generation had forgotten how to age properly.[29]

At the same time, however, modern medicine had to be given its due for measurable improvements. Hence Reveillé-Parise disputed the idea that the traditional countryside was healthier than the newer city, pointing out that peasants neglected proper hygiene and were poor and overworked. He and Noirot both rejected the Biblical claims, contending that each Biblical year was a mere three months in modern terminology. Average lifespan was in fact slightly higher than in the past, despite the popular tendency to exaggerate the vitality of earlier ages. But having said this both manuals went on to undermine their own hypothesis. Noirot blasted modern education as detrimental to long life: 'A precocious education kills in their buds the highest aptitudes of life and exhausts the sacred source.' He added that farmers, with their access to good air, lived longer than city workers. Noirot did admit that poverty was more detrimental to survival than wealth, but he repeated classical advice in noting that excessive wealth was itself a killer, not only through its support for overeating but also because of the monotony it caused. For Reveillé-Parise Paris was a jail, while the nineteenth century was turning everything to 'haste, hurry, torment,' all hostile to long life. Certainly the old should seek the peace of the countryside. A few students

of the centenarians contended that intellectuals lived longer than any
other category,[30] but most saw the poor peasant as the likeliest to
survive.[31] Few observers, then, even when they declared an official
optimism, really set the basis for compatibility between longevity and
the modern life-style. Many went on to add that the modern world
worsened the position of those who did reach old age. Chateaubriand
was one of many who, quite early in the nineteenth century, pointed
to those gloriously undefined 'old days' as a period in which the elderly
had been part of a community in contrast to their modern isolation.[32]

One thus emerges with a very callous image of old age. Assuming one
survived by rigid self-discipline, there was scant reward. The conventional
wisdom produced no reason to want to survive. The physical picture was
bleakest. At most it could be noted that some individuals experienced
a partial rebirth in their eighties, 'like those rare trees that flower again
in autumn, for the second time.'[33] Hence some attention was paid to
unusual phenomena such as a return of hair, menstruation and other
more or less desirable characteristics of younger adulthood. This
aside, the theme of decay, and attendant ugliness, was universal and,
in most accounts, given considerable detail.[34] For Reveillé-Parise, the
centenarian was a 'ruin of himself,' a mere vegetable. Old age was a
total transformation of the organism. Even the most optimistic could
only note that a few organs might be spared from loss of recuperative
ability. Old age was 'the retrograde period of human life, the age of
decline or of involution,' a state 'midway between disease and health,'
'the last, sad revolution which leaves only ruins behind.'[35] The theme
is a constant, from the late eighteenth century onward. The old could
only be pitied for their infirmities but even this was qualified by
revulsion at the ugliness of a wrinkled, toothless creature.

But what of the mental state and special virtues of the elderly? Here
lay Cicero's consolation and Buffon's pleasure in age, and the
advantages were not ignored in the new literature of the nineteenth
century.[36] The *Gazette de Médecine,* strongly disapproving an essay
on the evils of old age, claimed that while the body aged the spirit
never did.[37] Reference to creative older people were common:
Michelangelo, Voltaire (who would have lived still longer if vanity
had not tempted him to take his final trip to Paris), and later Hugo.
'The old man, whose intelligence continues to glow like a torch, the
old man who still has productive energies, can guide men and create
and manipulate ideas, preserves his value.'[38] But here was already the
opening wedge of dispute, for the old genius was by definition
atypical. For the common run of humanity, a special kind of mental

activity had to be claimed. Noirot, granting bleakly that the old had
nothing more to hope for on earth, characteristically stressed the power
of memory, which could continue to entertain.

Experience was hailed as well.[39] The old might be less quick, less
open to innovation, but, as Reveillé-Parise put it, 'One cannot deny that
the essential mode of intelligence and of its infinite applications belongs
to mature age.'[40] Most important the aged were not distracted by
passions, since their very survival depended on serenity and their physical
decay left them no energy anyway. 'The moral side is the beautiful side
of old age. We cannot age without our physique losing, but also without
our morality gaining; it is a noble compensation.'[41] Hence the old were
counted upon for benevolence, patience, acts of charity, as well as a
self-knowledge impossible to youth. Calm, then, replaced passions
which might be held of little value anyway. Hopefully the old man
could serve a vital role also in guiding a respectful family.

This preservation of classical and religious wisdom must not be
belittled. But without meaning to simplify or unify the modern
experience unduly, it is obvious that the calm, resigned life of the mind
being urged was not calculated to make old age attractive to more
modern urban kinds of expectations, and it had never been accessible
to most older people anyway. The manuals that advised an interest
in science or history were simply not talking to the interests of the
bulk of the older population, a problem that still pervades contemporary
guidance literature. Ciceronian advice on contemplation perhaps might
benefit a retired postal employee but there is little evidence that it
usually does – which may reflect as much on Cicero as on the postal
service. Important also was the fact that few manuals even specified
what one's intelligence was to be exercised upon. By the turn of the
century some were picking up the theme that a happy old age
depended on a young, innovative spirit, open to new ideas and
interested in what was going on around, but this was not yet the
common approach. As late as 1924 the old were urged to be resigned,
neither optimistic nor pessimistic; they should accept the inevitable
and learn to die well.[42] And this from an observer who urged the
morality and intelligence of old age. The lack of focus in the praise of
the mentality of old people remained a serious handicap.

Furthermore, intellectual capacities were also subject to the image
of doom. Few guides could avoid dwelling on the mental drawbacks
of the elderly and some stressed them exclusively. The theme of
mental decay gained increasing precision as medical knowledge
increased. Old age was not benevolent in any form, physical or moral.

The old were selfish, wrapped up in their own concerns. They lost their memories as well as their creativity. They were avaricious; this vice was given extraordinary attention.[43] Here is a clear connection between the manuals and popular culture – and, admittedly, the behavior of some old people as well. In a property-conscious society, where inheritance was all, avarice was an easy sin to identify; it meant among other things that the old clung to property for support in a hostile world, possibly for self-identification. The only remedy, as we have suggested earlier from the pen of a peasant, was more timely death. The elderly were believed to have lost all their good sense, which is why no one would listen to them anyway. If they acted old, it was noted in the 1860s, everyone shunned them, and if they acted young everyone laughed at them.

There was no escaping the dilemma. The main thrust of the old age culture was that the aged were distinctively senile whether constructive or not. Michel Lévy, like most manual writers, while admitting that a few old people stayed alert, was forced to conclude that most saw their minds decay gradually, leading them to a vegetal existence cut off from the world. Reveillé-Parise was less aware of the dilemma of the old, although he too dealt with individual variation. He wanted to be on the side of Cicero and the angels. The old should be esteemed, their intelligence was of the kind appropriate for leadership roles, they should enjoy peace and honor in their age. But, inexorably, their brains did decay – 'The faculties of intelligence share equally in this universal deterioration' – and they were commonly victim of all the vices attributed to them.

One final attribute, on which there was universal agreement, no sex; after a life of moderation, abstinence. This was not a new admonition. Like most of the sexual advice for which the Victorians have been blamed, it had ancient lineage and simply achieved wider currency given the new interest in, but failure to rethink, the phenomenon of aging. It was admitted that some men could maintain sexual activity, and cases of an octogenarian siring a child by a young woman were noted with a certain Gallic pride. But the eroticism of the old was much more commonly condemned as both disgusting and unhealthy. This applied also to those menopausal women who experienced erotic dreams and appetites. Genital decay was an essential attribute of old age, though this seemed clearest for women. 'Old age begins with the cessation of the genital function.'[44] Even where capacity remained, the mind should rule the passions – here was one action for which the elderly were certainly responsible. There might be beauty in the result; with age, 'love takes on an entirely moral character, liberated from the servitudes of animality.'[45] More commonly, however, danger was emphasized, once 'the hour of genital repose has sounded.'[46] From 1807: 'Abuses of the hymen harm even the most robust people,'[47] and the author went on to excoriate the stereotypic dirty old man. From 1873: 'Like our hair, our desires should wither.'[48] From 1911: 'Each sacrifice to Venus is, for the old man, a spadeful of earth on his head.'[49] From 1931: No more sex after 60 or 65; 'the genital secretions should remain to the profit of the organism that produces them.'[50] And here of course was the basis of the admonitions, a combination of the conventional stigma placed upon lust on the part of older people and a belief that genital fluids were part of the vital essence, perhaps the vital essence itself. Folklore, as evidenced by hostility to remarriage, particularly of widows, and medical traditions easily combined here. Noirot, urging continence early, on behalf of 'the vital fund,'[51] went on to illustrate how much longer monks and neuters lived than the generality of mankind. His recommendations at least had an air of practicality. Men could keep active, as with hunting; it was no accident that Diana was goddess both of chastity and the chase. Women could knit. And for both sexes (one assumes, in default of the monastery or castration; here too, logic was not the strong point of manual writers who poured out their scattered tidbits of conventional wisdom) there was marriage. It was long noted that married people lived longer than single. Noirot had isolated the cause: 'By excluding the attraction of novelty, marriage shelters man from artificial overexcitement.'[52] Only a few guides, by the twentieth century, either extended the period before which sexual activity should stop or recognized that occasional intercourse, so long as spurred solely by natural desire, might be all right.[53]

It is not anachronistic to poke a bit of fun at the manuals' approach to sex, for again it countered interests that steadily increased with modernization. But the recommendations on sex are just an extreme example of the general approach: no rethinking of the canons of behavior for older people and therefore a growing gap between what was desirable, indeed what was probably practised by some, and what was advised. The gap had potentially tragic consequences, for clearly many old people acted upon the advice. The conventional wisdom created few reasons for wanting to live to old age and thus enhanced the difficulty of adjustment for those who, usually to their surprise, reached that state.

And if little was offered to the elderly in general, absolutely nothing

was held out for the stronger sex. A few functions might be found for
old men, but none for women. There was, of course, the problem
of explaining the well-known fact that women lived longer than men,
though all the manuals proudly noted that the very old, the centenarians,
and the really creative among the elderly at any age were all male.
Women engaged in less physical labor, competition, and war; for some
writers this explained their edge. Or maybe it was because they talked
more, which preserved their interest in the little things of life. Or
because they were more sedentary — which allowed them to use less
oxygen — more sober and less ambitious, with no passions other than
love. Whatever the reason it was almost universally agreed that female
longevity was a disaster. A few commentators reverted to the plea
for morality. The obvious physical losses entailed in menopause might
be compensated by ethical gains; friendships might be more easily
formed when sexual rivalry was absent. But this was a slender reed, for
morality while desirable for men was essential for women and few
seemed sure they could bear the burden. Hence Dr Pinel, early in the
nineteenth century, noted menopause as 'most sad and melancholy. . .if
an elevated character does not replace, by pure enjoyments, the reign
of frivolous pleasures and the attractions of a dissipated life.'[54]
Menopause was certainly the key to the dilemma: 'nature refuses her
one part of the attributes of her sex.' 'An old woman is for nature only
a degraded being, because she is useless to it.'[55] The obvious basis of this
view was the association of life forces with sexual functions; women
began to age sooner, more definitely than men did. Relatedly aging
early marked the appearance of women. The theme of ugliness was
extremely pervasive, for the menopausal woman was held likely to be
obese, wrinkled, with deteriorated skin and hair. Reveillé-Parise, whose
professional work was mainly among old women, found their
appearance 'disgraceful,' though he admitted that a few looked good
with white hair.[56] Furthermore, it was assumed that bad appearance
bothered women more than men, because of their earlier
commitment to successful flirtation. 'In general one can divide the life
of women into three periods: in the first, they dream of love; in the
second, they make it; in the third, they regret its passing.'[57] Of course,
it was possible to point out the functions the grandmother could
preform in the family, with maternal affection replacing youthful ardor;
and religion was widely urged. But few would have disagreed with
Reveillé-Parise that, for women, 'old age is a terrible period.'[58] It began
early for women, whom nature then cruelly allowed to outlive men.

   The special judgments on women confirm the general

inappropriateness of the guidance given to older people well into the twentieth century. That portion of the population most likely to survive was left virtually functionless, indeed derided. Here too, the conventional wisdom, if unusually harsh in France, remained virtually unchanged. Manuals in 1920 would differ little from those of 1820, which is why some can range freely over a century or more in citing examples of common views. It was in fact in 1920 that Lacassagne's pamphlet stated starkly that most people who lived to 70 were physical and mental wrecks and wished they were dead.

It is clear, then, that France, far from being a source of admiration for patriarchs, or even tolerant of matriarchs, maintained an official culture that held old age in pity perhaps, but in scant respect. As already suggested, countries with a less traditional culture, even a culture that can with some qualifications be termed youth-oriented, might produce a more varied, if not completely contrasting, approach. It was in the 1920s that a spate of optimistic, if perhaps unrealistic, pamphlets began to appear in the United States urging the infinite number of activities open to old people. But what of the relation between the culture expressed in old age manuals, often backed by the authority of 'science', and actual outlook? If the preservation of classical admonitions was increasingly irrelevant to the urban, modernizing experience, they had continuing impact nevertheless, for middle-class readers of manuals often believed what they read; they could easily think, for example, that urban life would poison their old age even if they could not afford to escape it. And we have suggested a parallel popular culture, which was not caused by reading but which stemmed from many shared assumptions.

Signs of persistence of the popular culture abound, even when we stress the most advantaged social groups, even as we move to the present day. The culture had ample resonance in more general literature aimed at the middle classes. The *Gazette des Femmes,* in 1841, faithfully reproduced the notion that aging had deteriorated compared to the past, in part because of the modern woman's disgusting rage for cosmetics. Grandmothers were used as figures of sage advice, to be sure, but even in this literary ploy, grandma (by her sixty-sixth year) carefully refused to disclose her age, lest she shock her younger advisees.[59] The religious motif, more common in the magazines than in old age manuals, might lead to a greater stress on the ageless soul,[60] but otherwise there was little difference in the culture; in fact it could lead to attacks on any effort to prolong life. Even an article specifically on cosmetics noted that once one was fifty, there was no hope, 'no

way to repair the irreparable outrage of the years.'[61] Truly, as another
article noted, while praising the grandmotherly role, 'The people dethrone
kings and time dethrones women.'[62] There is no reason, judging by
widely read magazines, to disagree with Reveillé-Parise, who noted that
the general opinion associated age only with illness and imminent death,
expecting no enjoyment in it; even many older people, in his view, held
this outlook.[63] As an article in the *Revue des deux mondes* put it a
half-century later, 'One cannot hope to become old. It should be easier
to die with some hope left.'

But for our purposes the more significant point is the persistence of
these attitudes well into the twentieth century. They were to be seriously
qualified after World War Two, but even now they reappear. A doctor
in 1950, although noting some medical advance, including hormonal
treatments that might, just might, allow women to enjoy sex after
menopause, concluded that the old are cautious and selfish as their
brain atrophies faster and faster after the onset of age. Pension groups,
particularly between the wars, repeated the same laments, undoubtedly
with an eye toward public sympathy but with an undercurrent of self-
conviction as well; hence one magazine stated that even before sixty
many people had lost their strength, and this in a magazine that was
actually offering its readers gardens for sale, vacation plans, and the like.[64]
Somewhat more optimistically *La Vieillesse heureuse* returned to Cicero,
in 1956; admittedly the elderly had no strength save their morality, but
this should give them wisdom and authority which in turn merited the
regaining of traditional respect. Certainly the medical view was widely
accepted: 'Old age is a mosaic of deterioration.' *Troisième Age,* now
the largest periodical aimed at older people, began in its first year, 1959,
with the plea for automatic retirement at age 60, which would allow
France to have a young labor force and recognize the fact that the old
are incapable of heavy responsibilities and fatigues.

This view was to change, but it was amplified in this first statement:
aging begins at 48, the critical period; stabilizes a bit in the decade after
55, then becomes full of anxiety and deteriorating health; only at 72
comes serene incapacity, which leads calmly to death. With the same
kind of contradiction that was now developing in public self-perception,
the journal in the same year stressed that the 'life of old people is
worth living' but that the industrial revolution had destroyed the
affectionate family which had placed the elderly at the center of its
love. General MacArthur was also cited, to compound the complete
lack of consistency, on the possibility of an active, productive life into
one's seventies and eighties. But MacArthur had yet to conquer France

and he had never promised to return there; more pervasive, in the magazines produced to an extent for the elderly, was the traditional pessimism, at least until the 1960s, as in the case of journal that pleaded for sympathy for those over sixty, 'at the age when one can no longer do anything.' 'Old age is the sad age when everyone, recalling what he was and thinking of what he's become, measures his deterioration and suffers.'[65]

The opinions of organs of retirees form a probable framework for the outlook of the old themselves. In 1927, retired teachers in the Creuse established an *amicale,* which put out a tiny periodical bulletin noting how little participation they were able to solicit. (Again, the contrast with the United States, where retirees' groups became active before 1900, is marked; a cultural difference is inescapable.) The old in France simply did not view themselves capable of active association, and some were even fearful of any deviation from the daily routine. Many healthy retirees stayed away from the annual banquet, claiming that the food and excitement (shades of Galen) would hurt their health. The organization's leader urged against this, noting that all diets were provided for and a calm atmosphere was maintained to aid digestion. But even his own pitch suggests the deep roots of the traditional outlook toward age. What did one do at the banquets? See old friends of course, but mainly recall one's youth, 'which gives the illusion of reliving a bit the bygone days' and lets one forget for just a moment the routine of suffering and mourning. There were even some jokes, though of course no one laughed uproariously, just mildly; the charm of the occasion was a bit 'melancholy.' But next year — for things were changing — there was going to be singing, and maybe someday the group would dance as they used to when they were young.[66]

Here, admittedly in a single example, we catch the poignancy of the situation of the elderly, even teachers, some of whom might retire at 55. The culture had penetrated deeply, and even those who began, toward the teens of this century, to propose the first organizations of retirees, shared much of the outlook of debility. Even more of their colleagues failed to join at all, which produced local groupings, even in the 1960s, claiming no more than 110 members (under 1 percent of the retirees in the region) less than half of whom ever showed up for any activity.[67] Hence the accurate claim: if the old unite, 'by their number they can defend their rights;' but the sad admission that most remained isolated, believing that they were impotent to defend themselves.[68] The interwar period did spur associations of retirees, because the pressures of inflation and then depression created obvious and horrendous problems for people on fixed pensions. But almost none was formed among any group save state functionaries, despite the existence of a host of private plans. And even the functionaries were often led by men still on the job, whose motives, as we shall see were mixed.[69] When we look at retiree efforts *per se,* the more common picture is that of the *Fédération générale des retraités, section de l'Ain.* Begun in 1935 with 30 members, it had constant problems finding leadership and had grown to but 200 members even by 1957. Nancy claimed greater power, arguing in 1934 that it had 800 members; but it could muster only 200 people for a demonstration for a pension increase.[70] Thus promptings to join, even in a period of great crisis, vastly exceeded actual growth of organizations. The fact that organizations did spring up and find some support should not be minimized; for individuals this could signal a real change in one's sense of the possibility of an active role in modern society. But far more, the history of organizations agitating specifically even for the middle-class elderly reflect, again, the common outlook which the old apply to themselves, resulting here, to paraphrase a well-known title, in a culture of political despair. As one retired engineer said four years ago: 'At my age, what should I do with my little voice?'[71]

And there is little doubt that this sense of impotence was and is greater in France than in countries like the United States, which operated from a more open, or at least more ambiguous, set of attitudes toward the elderly. The French lagged even in the formation of groups for art work, sewing and the like, designed for the elderly. The first significant citations of such groups (obviously not precluding quite informal ones, among friends, far earlier) come in the 1950s,[72] and the common formation of 'Third age clubs' is literally but a few years old.[73] A 1965 survey of retired functionaries found 80 percent spending most of their time at home, though half claimed to want (but lacked) an active club where they could meet people.[74]

A sad picture, and one which suggests, accurately I think, that vital aspects of behavior, particularly until very recently, reflect the fact that the elderly held much the same view of themselves that the pervasive culture advised them to. They were ugly, selfish, impotent, and had best stay out of sight; their health was extremely fragile even if there were no overt symptoms of specific disease; so for a host of reasons organizational activity would be a danger and a waste.

This, then, is theme one suggested by the traditional culture.

Widely-shared attitudes persist and cause behavior; insofar as they are promulgated by popular and/or authoritative publications, they find reinforcement, but the roots go deep into fear of aging and hostility to the old. They long dominated the outlook of those who dealt with the elderly; this we will shortly see in discussing groups as diverse as medical researchers and radical labor leaders. They continue to overwhelm the old themselves in many social groups, particularly the lower classes; this also we will return to shortly.

But there is an irony in the culture toward aging, as expressed in manuals and general magazine articles. After World War Two it did a somersault. The basic message now is that age can be conquered. Old people are urged to avoid the behavior of the traditional elderly: 'It's time to change this record. Act young and you will be young.' Travel is recommended and in general the old are prompted to be open to change: 'To depart from routine at our age is a very good way. . . of remaining young.'[75] Sex, once disdained with horror, is now strongly encouraged as normal and healthy. In retirement an old person can make a new life, develop new interests. Or if a person chooses to continue to work his capacities will remain considerable. The very definition of age has changed; in a typical reshuffling one manual views the years 48 to 60 as a time of transition, 60 to 78 or 80 as one of calm, 80 to 92 as active old age, with senility coming only after this.[76]

There are a number of reasons for this change in outlook. The American example is one. Much of the new literature is copied from the United States, since the outpouring of happiness material has continued since the 1920s. Beauticians urge their female charges to copy the exercising, face lifting, and cosmetic practices of American women. While one proudly proclaims that France alone shares with the United States the honor of having a 'third woman,' between old and young — a woman who by all appearances might be thirty just as easily as fifty-five — she also bemoans the three centimeter edge in hip slimness that the average American woman preserves over her French counterpart.[77] The general openness of older Americans to sports, travel, and retirement groups is often commended.[78] Also praised is the presumed American practice of regular medical checkups, which as we will see began to be urged in France only recently. Greater American readiness to find interests even in their advanced years is perceived, however inaccurately, by the general public. One poll indicated considerable enthusiasm among French retirees to go to the United States to 'recycle,' though there is little evidence of practical follow-up to this interest.

Changes in French society bolster the new image. Medicine, though partly itself derivative, is one to which we turn shortly. The old are in fact more active, less ugly. The declining significance of property ownership as the basis of status and power is another factor of vital importance. An adjective that is never, now, applied to the old is miserly, despite its canonization from classical times onward. The young no longer have to wait for inheritance to begin their own adulthood. Generational tension remains but this fundamental feature of agricultural and traditional-burgeois society is gone. It is easier to feel responsible for one's parents, even reluctantly, than to hope for their death. Not coincidentally, whereas in the mid-nineteenth century on a *per capita* basis a person over fifty was four times as likely as a member of any other age group to be murdered (forming, despite their small size in the total population, the largest group of murderees), old people now comprise the smallest group of murder victims.[79] Straws in the wind, perhaps, but indications of a real correspondence between the change in the tone of the literature devoted to old age and actual social behavior, even in its less extreme manifestations.

Yet the basis for the new literature lies primarily in new behavior developed by old people themselves, particularly among the elements of the middle class. The existence of the new literature guides us to a more fundamental evolution in the outlook held by many older people and, to some extent, by those who deal with them. We must of course be attentive to the persistence of traditional motifs, for such a deep-rooted culture cannot die within a single generation. And it is premature to say that the evolution of the elderly in modern society, after over a century of gloom, has had a happy ending. The relationship between the new literature, easy to trace in its joyous acceptance of old age, and the actual outlook of older people, must preoccupy us as we essay an account of how the elderly have actually evolved in subsequent sections. Neither traditional pessimism nor recent optimism exactly hits the mark. There is movement, however, there is transition, won against the painful odds posed by customary assumptions, and this shows in most though not all of the social facets of aging. Even partial breakthroughs, against undiluted pessimism, can only be welcome.

Notes

1. Evelyne Sullerot, 'Woman's Role in Modern Society from the Sociological and Economic Point of View,' in Regional Trade Union Seminar, *Employment of Women* (Paris, 1968), p.91.
2. Evelyne Sullerot, *Women, Society and Change* (New York, 1974), p.46.
3. Fernand Boverat, *Le Vieillissement de la population* (Paris, 1946).
4. P. Flourens, *De la Longévité humaine* (Paris, 1854), p.39.
5. See also de Parcieux, *Essai sur les probabilités de la durée de la vie humaine* (Paris, 1746).
6. A. Lacassagne, *La Verte Vieillesse* (Lyons, 1920).
7. H. Guéniot, *Pour Vivre Cent Ans* (Paris, 1931), pp.26ff.
8. J.H. Reveillé-Parise, *Traité de la Vieillesse hygiénique, médical et philosophique* (Paris, 1853), pp.77-8.
9. Charles Vidal, *Le Vieillard* (Paris, 1924), pp.11ff.
10. I am grateful to Rudolph Bell in his paper 'The Persistence of Fatalism and its Demographic Base in Modern Rural Italy' and other works in progress, for these insights.
11. Reveillé-Parise, *Traité*, p.383.
12. P.L. Jacob, 'Conseils aux femmes sur la conservation de leur beauté,' *Journal des Femmes* (1843), pp.167, 461; see also Janine Alaux, *101 Trucs pour vaincre le coup de vieux* (Paris, 1973).
13. L. Noirot, *L'Art de Vivre Longtemps* (Paris, 1868), p.272.
14. Vidal, *Vieillard*, p.82.
15. Lacassagne, *Vieillesse*, 322.
16. André Léri, *Le Cerveau sénile* (Lille, 1906), pp.3-4 and *passim*.
17. Reveillé-Parise, *Traité*, pp.270ff.; see also Lacassagne, *Vieillesse*, ix.
18. Dr Scheffler, *Comment on défend sa jeunesse* (Paris, n.d.), p.35.
19. G. Rauzier, *Traité des Maladies des vieillards* (Paris, 1909), pp.14ff.
20. Elie Metchnikoff, *Etudes sur la nature humaine* (Paris, 1903), p.339.
21. Rauzier, *Traité*, *passim*.
22. Charles Legoncourt, *Galérie des centenaires anciens et modernes* (Paris, 1842), p.114.
23. Paul Carton, *Le Guide de la vieillesse* (Paris, 1951), pp.30ff.
24. *Gazette de médecine* (1861), p.74.
25. Noirot, *Art*, p.64.
26. Ibid., p.290.
27. Rauzier, *Traité*, p.324.
28. Carton, *Guide*, *passim*.
29. For more fundamental optimism see Jean Finot, *La Philosophie de la longévité* (Paris, 1900), p.42; A. Lorand, *La Vieillesse, Moyens de la Prévenir et de la combattre* (Paris, 1914). This last work, translated from the German, was notably more advanced than French medical treatises in its openness to possibilities of cure, its recommendations for regular sexual activity and so on; but it maintained the greater health of rural over urban people. Doubtless the fact that doctors rarely saw rural patients aided this impression, as did the widely current cultural prejudices against the city.
30. M. Philibert, *L'Echelle des Ages* (Paris, 1968), p.199.
31. Alfred Sauvy, *Les Limites de la vie humaine* (Paris, 1961), p.12.
32. Reveillé-Parise, *Traité*, p.69.
33. E. Monin, *Hygiène, et médecine journalière* (Paris, 1823), p.363.
34. Michel Lévy, *Traité d'hygiène publique et privée* (Paris, 1844), I, p.114.
35. M.A. Legrand, *La Longévité à travers les ages* (Paris, 1911), p.194.
36. Noirot, *Art*, p.256.

37. 'Les Peines de la vieillesse,' *Gazette de médecine* (1863), p.219.
38. Reveillé-Parise, *Traité*, p.92; see also Emile Demange, *Etude clinique et anatomie pathologique sur la vieillesse* (Paris, 1886).
39. Flourens, *Longévité*, p.54.
40. Reveillé-Parise, *Traité*, p.16.
41. Lacassagne, *Vieillesse*, pp.282-3.
42. Vidal, *Vieillard*, p.103.
43. J.A. Millot, *La Gérocomie* (Paris, 1807), p.98.
44. August Lumière, *Sénilité et Rajeunissement* (Paris, 1932), p.139.
45. Guéniot, *Pour Vivre*, p.71.
46. Noirot, *Art,* pp.227-8.
47. Millot, *Gérocomie,* p.98.
48. Noirot, *Art,* p.243.
49. Legrand, *Longévité,* p.147.
50. Guénoit, *Pour Vivre,* p.71.
51. Noirot, *Art,* pp.143ff.
52. Ibid., p.243.
53. Charles Vidal, *Etude médical, physiologique et philosophique de la femme* (Paris, 1912), p.143.
54. Ph. Pinel, *La Médecine clinique* (Paris, 1802), *passim;* Millot, *Gérocomie,* p.360.
55. *Gazette de Santé* (An 13), p.123; for an early expression of the standard view, C.A. Goubelly, *Connoissances nécessaires sur la grossesse, sur les maladies laiteuses, et sur la cessation des règles* (Paris, 1785), II, pp.362ff.
56. Reveillé-Parise, *Traité,* p.59.
57. Ibid., p.63.
58. Ibid., p.137.
59. *Gazette des Femmes,* 12 June 1841.
60. *Revue de la famille,* 15 April 1875.
61. Jacob, 'Conseils,' pp.164ff.
62. Anais Ségalas, 'La Vieille Femme,' *Journal des femmes* (1847), p.554.
63. Reveillé-Parise, *Traité,* pp.108, 137.
64. *Cri du retraité,* 1930 and 1934.
65. *Echo de la Vieillesse,* 1958.
66. *Bulletin trimestriel de l'Amicale des retraités de l'enseignement public du Creuse,* 1933.
67. *Annuaire des retraités des organismes sociaux de la région Montpellier-Languedoc-Rousillon,* 1960.
68. *Bulletin du département de Seine-et-Oise,* 1933; *Tribune des fonctionnaires,* 1926ff.
69. *Cri du retraité, passim.*
70. *Bulletin trimestriel du groupement des retraités civils de l'Est,* 1934.
71. Anne Lauran, *L'Age scandaleux* (Paris, 1971), p.49.
72. *Echo de la Vieillesse,* 1958.
73. *Troisième Age,* 1972.
74. 'Les Cadres retraités vus par eux-mêmes,' *Revue française du travail* (1968). In terms of membership in formal associations of the elderly only 38 percent of French males and 18 percent of females could be listed in 1972, and these often inactive. Groups involving upper- and middle-class elements here, not surprisingly, as in other areas of activity could claim a distinct lead, but even here only a minority was involved.
75. Léon Binet, *Gérontologie et gériatrie* (Paris, 1961); Jean Daruc, *Vieillissement de la population et prolongation de la vie active* (Paris, 1958); René Berthier, *Nouvel age de vie* (Paris, 1973); M. Shrem,

Des Anneés, oui; Vieillir, Non! (Neuchatel, 1965).
76. P. Baumgartner, *Les Consultations journalières en gérontologie* (Paris, 1968), pp.79 and *passim*.
77. Alaux, *101 Trucs, passim.*
78. *Troisième Age, passim.*
79. For congenital pessimists it can be noted that, perhaps replacing murder, old people, particularly males and mainly in the 60-69 age group, are vastly disproportionate victims of automobile attacks upon pedestrians. (After 70 apparently there is greater acceptance of immobility, perhaps greater recognition of elderliness by drivers, and much more caution when the forces of stop and go encounter each other; *per capita* death rates by vehicular death go down dramatically), *Statistique de la France, Mouvement de la population,* 1952ff. For percentage murder figures, same source, 1856 to the present.

2 OLD AGE IN FRENCH WORKING-CLASS CULTURE

It would be tempting to see aging, like death, as one of those basic human phenomena that cut across class lines. Certainly many of the physical processes are part of a common human experience. And many studies of aging have treated the condition without much regard for social class.[1] But in modern society one of the main functions of social class has been to prepare a differential response to aging, just as in earlier times social stratification served significantly to differentiate the trappings of death. We will deal subsequently with other class responses to aging and its anticipation, including working-class variants. But here we do focus on the working class and an outlook, a behavior set, that developed in response to aging and that survives in many respects to the present day.

Workers were not people who read old age manuals. What we find in their attitudes is bleaker in fact than what the published culture prescribed. Workers *and their spokesmen* shared assumptions about aging, obviously mutually reinforcing, that have proved hideously unrealistic. From the standpoint of labor leaders, these attitudes may have related to general knowledge picked up from literature on aging. But more widely, and certainly among workers themselves, the outlook reflected a popular culture, self-generated and, as we have suggested, perpetuated from a rural past.

The problem can be stated starkly. Whereas large segments of the middle classes began to learn to prepare for aging in new ways during the nineteenth century, the working class did not. Much of this differentiation was initially rooted, of course, in material levels; workers lacked resources that the middle classes had. But more than this was involved, if only as a product of the material situation.

Workers expected to grow old early, by modern standards; what was middle age even to other contemporaries was old age to them. But more basically the concept of aging itself was foreign: one lived, deteriorated a bit, and died. The notion of a distinct period of life — quite apart from the problem of whether this began at fifty or sixty-five — was lacking. We have suggested the increase in the percentage of the population over sixty, from a probable 7 percent in 1778 to 15 percent in 1926.[2] In human terms this meant that individual families and institutions had to prepare to support older

people on an unprecedentedly slender demographic base. Low birth
rates meant that a clerk or a worker had few surviving children to look
to for support when old. French statistical publications graphically
detail the trend. By 1900 the average 65-year-old had 2.5 surviving
children. Shopkeepers exceeded the average, clerks were well under
(with 1.7), reflecting intraclass birth rate differentials. The still
massive agricultural population came close to 3. This meant that
urban workers hovered close to (indeed, in the case of skilled workers,
a bit under) the national average, at 2.7 in 1891 and falling. How
much worry did this cause? How keenly did workers feel the absence
of sure support from surviving children, given the fact that averages
obviously conceal many cases in which an aging parent saw his
children die or found them uncaring? Here is a major element of the
background to the modern history of working-class aging, not peculiar
to France but first realized there because of the early decline of birth
rates.[3]

Yet older workers seldom speak to us directly. They have virtually
no publications (railway workers, not all blue-collar, being the only
exception), they do not strike, they remain passive. This means that
we must use two sources primarily to trace their history. The first
consists of the pronouncements and behavior of labor organizations.
These are not necessarily representative of workers; indeed in key
cases they were definitely the contrary. They are interesting in
themselves, as despite myriad internal political disagreements they
almost invariably shared a culture toward working-class old age; here
we link with a bleak interpretation of popular beliefs as
already generally defined. The second involves records of worker behavior,
largely statistical but highlighted by a few comments by ordinary
workers in various contexts. We can emerge with a pretty good idea,
if not proof positive, of what most workers thought about old age
in advance and in the fact. Again the conclusion must be that a deep-
seated attitude toward aging had developed which continues to
influence behavior; and frankly, we can use history to suggest what
must be changed.

We find little trace, in the working-class culture, of veneration
for aging. We have raised this topic before, but now we can make it
more precise. Peculiar family habits of Western Europe singularly
limited the concept of old age. Peasants married late, which meant
that it was unlikely for a father or mother to live to be grandparents
for a significant period of time; when they died there would in fact
still be young children in the house.[4] If unexpectedly they lived to

the point where their oldest children pressed to assume full adulthood, including property control, intergenerational pressures could be intense, even if there was no need for a formal concept of retirement. Yet retirement was common; by the late nineteenth century, when precise figures are available, rural workers listed themselves as retired far more commonly than urban workers, and the same applied to rural small holders (55 percent retired at age 65) compared to urban shopkeepers. All this was informal, incomplete in the sense that the old farmer still tried to help out and direct a generation he often regarded as dangerously corrupt; but retirement existed in fact.

To be sure, if older people stayed in the countryside they would be listed as heads of household into the mid-twentieth century. This reflects more than census-takers' simplifications. The French government still blithely assumes that if you are old but rural you are working and integrated into your community. The facts can be otherwise. The son may run the whole show, with grandpa and grandma serving as baby-sitters and poultry tenders at best. But it looks good on the record, so this is what we are officially informed.

It is true as well that older people themselves rarely moved from the farm which accounts for much of the higher percentage of old people in rural areas compared to urban. But with industrial growth as even young people moved to the cities, they would eventually age, and here is the key working-class problem. By the late nineteenth century there was a massive urban elderly population. Yet when people moved to the cities from a rural heritage that did not prepare them for old age, hostile to many aspects of old age if they achieved it, they were severely and newly burdened. The decline in potential child support, though possibly not without its compensations as there was less clawing for property, was one aspect of change. Nevertheless, for the new propertyless proletariat this brutal fact was new: one could less easily retire, even in the messy, contentious fashion of the rural population, whether deliberately or not. In contrast to the numerous cases of peasant retirement, the urban proletariat overall had no sense or active expectation of quitting work unless absolutely disabled. There was little to offer one's progeny, however numerous, in return, in an environment still dominated by poverty. If disability or even affection prompted one to depend on a child, there was greater likelihood, given urban housing conditions, that this would mean direct coresidence, which prompted a new set of tensions; the city did not easily allow a worker to put grandpa in a cottage back of the main farm, where both generations might know a bit of independence. And, though not necessarily new as a problem or attitude, there was simply too much to do to get through one's working life to prepare for aging, which was either not expected — given the high rates of accident and mortality and the traditional expectations of death — or regarded with fear.

We catch poor workers in Lille, shortly before 1830, expressing their sense of powerlessness to prepare for senescence. 'When we grow old, we'll go to the hospital, or we'll die, and that will be that.'[5] Yet we know that the reference to hospital — the famous *hospice* which the French had long set aside for the old and incurable and from which one had scarcely better than half a chance of emerging alive — was little more than an expectation of death among strangers. Of course the working-class family gained more structure during the nineteenth century, and its extended quality gave hope for provision for older members though with potential problems to which we have already averred. Michael Anderson has pointed out that coresidence with married children was the only means by which the growing number of older workers could survive. Where working-class culture allowed married women to work, as in the textile areas, the older relative could make a positive contribution to the extended household, by baby-sitting.[6] But more commonly he or she was just a drain economically and, without much doubt, a severe burden emotionally. Contemporary evidence on the distaste with which coresidence is viewed within the working class, by children and older people alike, would apply just as firmly to the nineteenth century, when housing was still more exiguous and aging itself less expected.[7] Small wonder that German workers listed provision for their old age as their greatest concern in life. Yet the concern remained in important respects unfocused, because there was no encouraging culture for recourse. German workers could talk about their fears for old age, but they professed to leave to chance what would actually become of them: 'as God wishes,' or 'as the wind blows me' were pervasive sentiments. Oddly, in a country where social insurance was already well established, the notion of pensions was rarely mentioned.[8]

One faces again the tantalizing question of exactly what expectations about aging were brought in from the village. There are two logical possibilities: villagers had esteemed age but found the bases for esteem eroded in the new cities. This would coincide with much conventional and scholarly wisdom. Or villagers, despite or because of the presence of elderly among them, disdained the state and did not hope or expect to attain it. I find the latter hypothesis by far the more probable. This was a society surrounded by death and decrepitude, and the urban lower class largely perpetuated the culture that had resulted. But one can maintain this latter argument as the basis for popular outlook and still note the further pressures placed upon aging by the new city environment.

Customary attitudes toward aging were exacerbated by the experience of deterioration on the job itself that became a normal working-class career pattern. Unless protected by union seniority provisions — and these were ill-developed on the Continent and the United States until well into the twentieth century, and incomplete even in Britain — the workers in virtually any industry would expect earnings and skill levels to decline rapidly after the age of forty. Workers above this age found it difficult to get a new job of any sort, so they had to protect themselves by working assiduously without the relief which absenteeism or other forms of indiscipline could provide their younger counterparts. Frequently they were demoted; unskilled workers were normally older than the skilled group in a factory because they had been forced from this group as their physical capacities waned and their skills became outmoded. In terms of his work experience, then, quite apart from actual problems of health, the worker could only see life as a process of decline, with the peak coming tragically early.[9] This remains an important part of working-class culture, which is still defined largely in terms of physical strength; interviews in America continue to suggest a sense that life is best in one's early twenties, in contrast to the middle-class preference for the forties. Workers, with rare exceptions, had no retirement plans, which forced them to accept demotion and any other indignities necessary to maintain work. The middle class, richer, was developing plans, as we will see. Again we deal with a material fact, but something beyond. The difference stemmed not only from funds available but from outlook. Workers were caught in a vicious circle, in which old age was not expected, therefore not provided for, and thus, once attained, almost completely devoid of purpose. Lacking an understanding that they would age or preparing individual solutions for the problem, workers were not capable of raising the issue of old age problems on their own initiative. The lack of preparedness was in part due to the failure of their own labor organizations. Most logically one would expect union support for pension funds at the least. But the fact was that French labor groups were particularly hostile to pension plans, whether run by the groups themselves or sponsored by the state, for their ideological proclivities inclined them against benefit programs that would tie workers to the existing order. Even British unions, strong in their possession of pension funds, viewed these largely as means for provision for widows and orphans after death, not a distinctive way of approaching one's own old age; and British workers were no more likely than French actually to retire. Retirement was completely alien to working-class culture.[10]

Elements of the French government, along with some employers, were among the first to realize the dimensions of the demographic change at the older age categories. They were prompted by bourgeois humanitarianism, for the discussion of the decrepit worker still forced to cling to a job had grown up virtually with industrialization itself. (Diderot indeed had outlined a scheme of old-age insurance and medical care in the mid-eighteenth century; happily, due to the speed-up of the modern historical process, it took only two hundred years to approximate it.) For the industrialist, compassion might be involved but also the knowledge that a general plan might equalize competitive conditions, for a handful of companies had developed pension schemes that might be relieved by a state program; and behind this in turn a growing belief that older workers were a handicap and that a neat program that prompted them to contribute to their own retirement might aid the company itself. Pension plans were first being tossed into the legislative hopper by the 1880s, but taken seriously only in the ensuing decade. Given the new interest of the government and some industrialists the labor movement was forced ultimately to develop some position, and this gives us our first insight into aspects not just of socialist or syndicalist rhetoric, but of genuine working-class culture. The CGT and the major socialist groups prompted by the passage, in the Chamber of Deputies in 1896, of a draft pension law, were obliged to consider the old. The Marxist wing (the Guesdists) had earlier vowed to 'place the aged and the disabled at the charge of society,'[11] but this was in no way a subject commanding significant attention. Even the discussion of the late 1890s died down quickly, because the government itself dropped the subject, and interest revived only after 1906 when the matter came up again in Parliament — cresting in 1910-11 when the first pension law was passed. Pension issues in the meantime tended to be reserved for the end of a labor congress session; Niel, a former head of the CGT, blasted his colleagues because of their scanty and

intermittent attention to the whole question.[12] Again and again
labor's response was that pensions were very important but that
someone else should deal with the matter. The glassworkers' union
in 1903, for example, discussed with real feeling the dilemma of
older workers in the industry, who were often used up by their mid-
forties and were demoted or even fired. The obvious conclusion was
that an early retirement age was essential and that the state proposals,
which involved retirement at 65, were irrelevant. But having said
this, the delegates went on to admit that they had nothing to
propose themselves and would welcome someone else's initiative.
Fernand Pelloutier put the case in more ideological terms: 'It is not
up to the workers to indicate the means of assuring their old age;
the obligation is incumbent upon capitalist society.'[13] Something
of this mood carried through the whole history of pension
discussions. Individual unions tended to look to the CGT, or later the
Communist CGTU, for direction, often just repeating their formulas
if they discussed pensions at all. The CGT, at least after its most
active syndicalist phase, was inclined to rely on the Socialist, or
later the Communist, party for initiative. And the political parties,
though extremely active in the rare parliamentary debates on the
subject, seldom discussed the pension question thoroughly. This is
not to minimize the impact of organized labor's recurrent interest
in pensions; even in the 1910-11 laws, labor pressure induced
Parliament to lower the possible retirement age from 65 to 60. But
overall concern remained surprisingly dependent on outside
initiative.

To be sure, the economic intricacies of old age were not
comprehended; particularly among the unions, there was widespread
disinterest in the details of a viable pension plan. Even for their own
officials, important unions worked out pensions only *ad hoc,* as late
as the 1920s.[14] The textile workers' federation in 1920, noting its
lack of information on pension arrangements in a period of rising
prices, expressed the hope that the socialist deputies and the CGT
would take care of the matter. Particularly before World War One,
when syndicalist interest ran highest, fiscal details were eschewed in
favor of sweeping proposals. In 1901 a Saint-Denis union council
proposed a substantial pension program to be financed via the
abolition of the religious budget; reduction in military spending;
and elimination of spending on receptions for 'foreign potentates.'
If this did not suffice, dues might be levied on employers — really
a rather mild assault on the social order. Another suggestion

involved the nationalization of insurance companies; advocates admitted they had no idea whether the result would cover pension payments except to note that 'fantastic' capital was involved.[15] This inadequate approach resulted obviously from the leading concerns of the trade unions, which related first and foremost to work and wage, not to life after work, though a distinctively French ideological element cannot be denied. The general factors were these: political parties and unions alike looked to youth, for they believed not only in new members but the kind of vigor that would constitute the wave of the future, not the hesitations and nostalgia characteristic of old age. Hence the labor movement regularly reported only on youth activities, even as the work force in fact became older and older.

The special ideological factor initially derived from syndicalism, which prompted a belief that no reform was possible in bourgeois society and that only a future, revolutionary order 'will assure the division of production to take care of all the needs of those who can and should produce as well as those (children, invalids, the aged) who cannot and who have the absolute right to live comfortably.'[16] Lovely sentiments, but distressingly similar to the equation that bourgeois society has already adopted in lumping the same odd trinity in a single institution, the *hospice.* Here working-class culture was equivalent to educated medical culture. The old were disabled by definition. The ideology corresponded with more general workers' beliefs in one respect, that dues should not be levied, given the fact that workers did not earn enough to cover even present needs; society or the employers should pay. A special problem, which seems more specifically syndicalist, stemmed from state insistence, in good bourgeois fashion, of capitalization of the funds; the CGT wanted division of contributions *(répartition)* on an ongoing basis, and this is in fact the foundation of the present social security systems of most countries, though caused by the desire to keep pace with inflation more than to please any particular ideological group. But in the pre-1914 debates, the extent to which invested funds would tie workers to the existing order was a real problem, and contributed to the disinterest of the articulate labor movement in parliamentary, actuarial plans. [17]

Ideology also prompted interesting debate about the content of pension plans, and here we get closer to the outlook of the working class more broadly. The radicals (syndicalists and left-wing socialists) favored a low retirement age with high benefits, profiting of course from their unwillingness to discuss modalities. They insisted particularly that few workers lived to 65 anyway. In the SFIO congress of 1910, in which a major split opened on this issue between revolutionary socialists and syndicalists, on the one hand, and reformists on the other, Paul Lafargue argued vehemently that only 8 percent of the working class lived past 60; the reformists disputed this, but only one was expert enough to provide actuarial data. Lafargue and the revolutionaries were in fact seizing upon census statistics which indicated that only 8 percent of the population was *then* over 65, which was of course quite different from the life expectancy of an actual worker. The ethics and/or intelligence of such an approach may be questioned, but the conclusion was logical enough. The state plan was no good. Lafargue doubted that any assistance for older workers was needed, since they would all die so early; rather, protection of those still at work was essential.[18]

The SFIO in fact voted to support a pension law while working for steady improvements; by 1912 the CGT itself was taking a more moderate tone, talking in terms of the desirability of revising the law.[19] And of course reformists and even some radicals had long since argued that some law was better than none, and that pensions need not prevent the revolution. As early as 1891 the miners' union urged improved pension payments in their industry 'while awaiting society's acceptance of responsibility for the aged and invalids at work.'[20]

There is no doubt that many workers disagreed with the anti-pension approach, which is the main reason the CGT trimmed its sails so quickly; we will return to this point. But the radicals' arguments should not be dismissed too lightly, quite apart from the fact that they help explain the desultory attention which the whole aging question received from the main organs of the French labor movement.[21] The interest in youth, in people at work, showed up clearly and could characterize movements with a much more reformist approach. More basically some of the radicals' arguments reflected the penetration of the work ethic into the organized labor movement. The aged were lumped into a general category of unfortunate, because they could not or did not work or were degraded in their jobs. Many workers shared this view, as we shall see. Many workers also agreed that while pensions were desirable they could not afford to pay for them; here was one horn of a dilemma which the radicals exploited cleverly.[22] Many also agreed that few of their number would reach age 65. Their own experience, their sense of decrepitude as they aged, made it logical to mix thoughts of aging with thoughts of death.

And the radicals reflected as well as perpetuated the confusion about how to prepare for old age. Again there should be no mistaking the fact that workers wanted pensions, at least as they neared sixty and realized that they might, after all, survive for a while. But the radicals did appeal to some basic impulses about the aging process, and no doubt helped maintain them.

Yet the radical impulse was already irresponsible. It corresponded to what most workers had to do, that is, to continue working until they dropped, but not to what even a modest reconsideration of the situation of the elderly, such as the bourgeois state was proposing, could have produced. What was actually happening to diverse groups of older workers illustrated both the real and the possible.

Until after 1911, worker behavior, whatever their private beliefs, largely corresponded to the unions' policies. Pensions were no more mentioned in spontaneous strikes than in strikes with trade union involvement; indeed they were not raised as an issue in any setting of direct conflict. Most workers did not expect to retire and would ignore pension proposals unless retirement began in middle age. Those thousands of workers who did reach their fifties must have begun to realize that this pessimism was self-defeating, but they were not powerful in labor councils (their own view of the impotence of age still holds them back and prevents self-identification as a subgroup within the working class). And while, as their zeal for pensions under the 1911 scheme was to demonstrate, they were open to outside initiative, their own association of aging and death made them incapable of conceiving of an active plan on their own or to see retirement as anything but an immobile period in which death was awaited with resignation. Here of course was a vicious circle. Without state or private plans workers could not retire; as we will see, the contrast with those few groups whose organizations had developed a definite pension interest was striking. So most did work until they died or were disabled. The ability of many aged workers to plod on must have convinced many an employer that great concern about pensions was unnecessary, while many a worker, surprised at having survived, could only be pleased at his ability to continue self-support.

So most members of the working class who passed the age of 65 kept on working, and without collective complaint, until the 1911 plan, inadequate as it was, suggested something of an alternative. We are dealing here with an immensely inarticulate group, for few older workers spoke out as older workers. But even general statistics, allowing for huge margins of error, give us the dimensions of life. In the first place pension programs in private industry were virtually non-existent for blue-collar labor, and generally of such recent vintage that it would be years before they would have visible effect. An 1898 inquiry produced the following results: 96 companies outside mining and transport had pension plans, covering 74,000 of the 86,000 workers in the concerns involved (thus excluding casual labor, younger workers and so on; few women, also, were involved in these industries). The vast majority of participants were in metallurgy; the crafts offered almost nothing (600 construction workers were covered for example; 1,761 printers). To these should be added (against excluding mines, transport and commerce) 40,491 workers whose companies participated in the *Caisse nationale de retraites,* again with roughly the same distribution among industries.[23] In contrast under an 1892 law 146,500 miners had pension plans, though of course the recency of the schemes would delay impact on retirement. To this stark picture should be added the fact that many private programs provided not for fixed retirement, but for cases of invalidity only.

This sets the background for the grim reality of the situation of older workers. For contrary to the impressions we have recorded from the period, and which some historians seeking to commiserate with workers without actually studying them have tried to perpetuate, there were older workers within industry, thousands of them in fact.[24] Even in the mines workers were not automatically dead or disabled at 45; herein constituted the ironic problem. Furthermore, with some qualification to be introduced in a moment, employers did not automatically fire older workers, as some have claimed in their zeal to capture capitalist cruelty for French industrialization since its inception.[25]

In 1900, in the whole population, adult males aged 55 to 64 had an annual death rate of .93 percent; those 65 to 70, 1.33 percent, and so on.[26] We can assume that the rates for the working class were higher, and the following calculations arbitrarily double them. Nevertheless, even with this stipulation, only 10 percent of all workers 60 and over would die in a five-year period. Applying the formula resulting from probably surviving workers to mining, 54 percent of the labor force over 60 in 1901 was still at work (excluding those having probably died) at age 65 or over in 1906; in metallurgy the figure was the same. In both cases the existence of some pension plans plus devastatingly hard work pushed or enticed a large minority into retirement. But in French manufacturing overall, 65 percent of all men and 69 percent of all women, again

having excluded the 10 percent mortality group, persisted. Domestic
manufacturers persisted at a 74 percent rate. Few factory or shop
industries departed significantly from the national average: printing,
with 59 percent, showed a possibly greater sense of and possibility of
retirement, though also, conceivably, the effects of lead poisoning
and skill displacement. Metals stood at 65 percent, construction at
63 percent, textiles at 67 percent, wood at 68 percent, and so on. In
other words the average worker labored until death or disability
terminated the career. And with the partial exception of printers the
labor aristocracy, the group most sophisticated in seeking benefits
on and from the job, showed no lead in retirement initiation. Again,
retirement was not seen as a realistic goal, possibly not even as a
desirable goal for it would end one's creative life. But all workers
suffered in seeking to remain in the labor force. A disproportionate
number were unemployed. Illness and displacement show their hand
here, as in 1906 the unemployment rate of males over 60 stood a
full 100 percent above the average. Both causing and resulting from
this pressure, still more people entered the ranks of the unskilled
in their later years. Again, census figures catch this movement only
in a gross sense. But in 1911 only 1 percent of all French printers
were over 65, only 2 percent of all male metal-workers. Juxtaposed
with the persistence figures cited above this means that many workers
abandoned such trades even before old age, or rather found old age
affecting them early, before 55. Textiles were a bit more generous, to
men and women alike, for here the percentage stood above the
average for all manufacturing, at 3.7 percent. But the concentration of old
people was disproportionately among the unskilled, with 59 percent
of all general laborers (and therefore 29 percent of all employed
males in manufacturing and transport in this age group) recording
ages over 65. Old people had to work; a surprising number survived;
but many had to accept declining pay and degradation of skill
given the absence of any planned treatment of their survival. Some,
though now unskilled, worked as watchmen; but others in the general
laborer category were forced into strenuous jobs that could only
complicate the physical problems of aging. Small wonder that when
retirement became a more active possibility, with the 1911 law,
workers compelled their leaders to accept any crumbs the state would
offer.[27]

In France as a whole in 1901, 69 percent of all males over 65
were employed or seeking work. In other words the factory labor
group should not be isolated as subject to peculiar discrimination.

Fifty-four percent of all agricultural employers worked, and while there is a persistent assumption that a bit of plowing at an advanced age keeps one feeling healthy and socially integrated the same might apply to some factory workers in their respective jobs as well. (Interestingly, only 38 percent of male agricultural workers persisted.) Sixty-four percent of males in liberal professions kept on working, 196 percent of women in the clerical professions (this startling figure reflecting the rapid growth of white-collar work as well as the desperate plight of single or widowed females, even less likely than males to have pensions or adequate savings). In general, retirement was abnormal, and only a few small groups were pioneering its development. It was not strange that most workers did not contemplate retirement as an active possibility. This would correspond not only with the absence of resources which would allow retirement, but with the absence of a sense of what one would do without work in a period when even the young found it difficult to define new uses for leisure time[28] and, of course, the persistent problem of realizing that one was going to reach old age at all.

This, then, was the majority situation; but the minority deserves attention as well. Thirty-one percent of all French males over 65, and 35 percent of all working-class males, were not listed as employed. We have noted that this did not preclude part-time jobs, which could provide funds and also a continuing sense of ties with the active life of younger days. Was the retired minority disabled, eking out survival on public charity and the grudging support of their families? Or, beneath the surface of working-class culture, were they developing a more positive sense of retirement? The question can be posed far more readily than answered. Certainly only a handful were in public institutions, the *hospices* for the old and infirm that had been so long and justly dreaded as places to go and die alone. Between 1897 and 1905 only 3 percent of the population over 60 were in such institutions. In these years those who entered could expect to remain, on the average, 260 days a year (250 for males) and a fifth would die annually (20.5 percent for males, 18.8 percent for females). So it was well to stay out. As to more general public aid — gifts of food and, more rarely, money from the *bureaux de bienfaisance* and medical aid provided for the indigent over 70 (consisting of money grants of up to 100 francs a year) — industrial departments like the Nord annually aided 1.7 percent of all inhabitants over 60 with charity aid grants in the period; more commonly industrial departments hovered nearer 1 percent, while most rural departments aided but

0.3 percent. The medical aid was more extensively sought, although its utilization varied madly without correlation to industrial concentrations. Thus in 1909 47 percent of all people over 70 in Corsica received some aid, 37 percent in the Nord and the Bouches-du-Rhône, 21 percent in the Rhône, and so on; the overall national average was 20 percent. This, it should be noted, was a new program, launched by a 1905 law.[29] Previously free medical care given to those over 60 (taking an annual average from 1899 to 1904) had benefited but 12 percent of the relevant age group each year.

In other words, not surprisingly, institutional aid, apart from its meager quality, cannot explain how the minority of retired workers got through their lives, even if we assume, as is reasonable, that they used the relevant facilities more frequently than the population as a whole.[30] A bit of aid plus an occasional job helped, but two other options predominated. First, living with younger relatives, particularly if baby-sitting services could benefit the elderly economically by freeing the young mother for work and/or where disability prevented remunerative employment. This pattern had been studied for the working class in other countries[31] and obviously has applicability to France.[32] Working-class mothers in particular could expect to live in their eldest daughter's household. In contrast, the final alternative: return to the countryside. With a bit of money saved, possibly with some scrap of pension, with some assistance from more distant relatives in a village of origin, one might escape the city and use cheaper rural life as a first kind of real working-class retirement. Not an exciting invention perhaps, indeed backward-looking in some respects, but one which finds statistical support for the period. In 1891 Paris had 34 percent of its inhabitants over 60, compared to the number in the 40-49 age group (this latter a fairly decent control mechanism, if a rough one, since it postdates the most active immigration); cities with populations over 100,000 had 39 percent, those 30,000-100,000 45 percent, France overall 44 percent. Particular departments like the Eure definitely show increases in the population over 65, or at least relatively small decreases, that strongly suggest movement from industrial cities — clerks no doubt, but some workers too.[33] Yet the movement from cities was too small to account for more than a tiny minority of workers not listed as continuing on the job; familial aid in the city loomed larger.

In sum the minority of retired workers included some desperately poor, although low use of the more detested state aid facilities cautions us against exaggerating their number. Only in ill health, after the 1905 law encouraged aid to people outside institutions, did even 70-year-olds begin to turn to collective support in significant proportions. Far more received private help, especially from their families, though they might live in independent households. Within this group some realized a first form of genuine working-class retirement, if this word means anything more than cessation of regular employment: they went back to the country.[34] Their effort depended heavily on individual resources and initiative, even if the rural haven was a traditional one. Prior savings, the sense that fishing and gardening would provide a pleasant means of ending one's days, hint at the only kind of culture that could dent the otherwise pessimistic view that workers and their representatives took of the entire aging process. Maybe if one could escape work and return to the soil the rest and peace that a worn-out laborer alone could endure might be possible.

We cannot glorify this group of early working-class retirees as pioneers on a new path of solace for old age. We do not know enough about what they did to say if retirement had positive connotations or was forced upon them by employers and/or disability, although we will make a more precise stab at this subsequently. Some undoubtedly carved out the calm, possibly diversified life that fits one's image of desirable repose after a life of labor. Many depended on family, as we will show in later discussion of patterns of residence; this could be a rewarding grandparental experience or relegation to a begrudged, tiny room. Above all, the retirees must be remembered as a minority, whether envied or ignored by the majority who continued work. Retirement, once more, was not a generalized working-class concept unless suggested from the outside. Work, even at declining pay and increasing degradation, was the norm.

As will be shown more fully later, middle-class groups alone were able/wanted to retire; male white-collar workers retired at a 94 percent rate between 60 and 65 in government service between 1901 and 1906, and 23 percent did so even in private manufacturing. More relevant to our class analysis is the case of railroads. Railway workers had a strong state pension plan, and in this same census period only 20 percent of the probably surviving workers continued in their jobs. They might continue unrecorded work as auxiliaries, for their pensions were not high and some people were really loath to abandon work entirely; others, lost in the anonymous census figures, may have entered some other full-time job. But we can assume that a good portion did retire, often remaining in a small

town, where they previously worked as signalman, or migrating to
the countryside, where in fact a few specific retirement homes existed
(almost unique for the French working class), although small.

This actual behavior pattern relates to union policy, where we can
add a couple of other odd groups. It can be no surprise that organized
white-collar workers saw pensions as one of their main goals. Indeed
initial CGT willingness to discuss this subject at all was attributed to
small unions of journalists and municipal employees. Teachers soon
joined them, wanting freedom to retire at 55 and an increased pension
rate any time salaries went up. 'The pension will be sacred because
we've acquired it, or will acquire it by our contributions.'[35] Postal
workers were equally vigorous. They too pressed to keep their pensions
attuned to the cost of living, particularly during the inflationary
interwar years. Like the teachers they saw the pension as a right, and
typically wanted to get at it as early as possible. And following from
this attitude, functionaries have long maintained the earliest retirement
age in France. These white-collar workers manifested an even more
basic distinctiveness in their attitude toward aging, for they fought
for a notion of steady advancement until retirement. Aging at work
for the employee was a normal progression to higher responsibilities
and higher pay. Firm retirement plans followed from this approach,
and the relevant unions paid great attention to advancement and
pensions alike.[36] It seems clear that many white-collar workers
expected to live to retirement and planned not only to support
themselves but to make life interesting after retirement. We will note
some qualifications to this characterization, but on balance class
differences in the approach toward aging emerge strongly within the
union movement.

But the same pattern developed with blue-collar workers who had
an 'in' with the government. Wherever blue-collar personnel had or
developed some special contact with the state, their unions quickly
elaborated pension proposals. Railroad workers, who admittedly
included a white-collar element, even shared the concern for regular
advancement by seniority in jobs. The other groups — miners,
merchant seamen, and tobacco and match workers — did not depart
from normal patterns in this regard and even the railway workers
shared the working-class pessimism about old age, but they did have
their pensions. All felt free, quite early, to launch a policy of demanding
steady improvements in the scheme that covered them. Miners could
refer to a decree from Henry IV promising pensions; their union began
agitating for an effective system in 1883, and the relevant law was

passed in 1894. Even the syndicalist miners' union accepted the law, working for its extension to slate miners and, of course, its general improvement. Merchant seamen pointed to Colbert's pension scheme for them, and as they unionized they pressed for higher benefits under it, again negotiating directly with the government. Railway unions and public utility workers dealt with private concerns for the most part, but they could refer to conditions on the state line or to public responsibility for conditions where monopolies had been granted; the railway workers came directly under legislation. Match workers offer a similarly interesting case, for they had no special claim to, or apparent concern for, pensions until their companies were nationalized in 1890. Immediately they came under a state pension system, and their union busily negotiated for improvements and handled individual complaints where pensions did not correspond to expectations. In all these industries workers pressed for a lowering of the retirement age (to 45 in mining, to 55 in match manufacture) and for higher benefits before 1900.[37]

Why did access to the government open the way to such intense and articulate attention to the material problems of retirement? There is no question that the government was a softer touch than private industry; postal workers, for example, were covered by a law of 1855. Association with the state allowed workers who were personally inarticulate about the prospect of aging to grasp a concrete plan; once they had this they could easily agitate for improvements. There was no objection to dues-paying in this situation. State initiative thus converted vague worry, the 'where the wind blows one' syndrome, into belief in retirement. Furthermore some of the industries involved attracted workers especially careful to provide for their old age. Railroad recruitment, for example, drew from explicit applicants, and pensions were one of the attractions. Again, however, interest was more general, for applicants for railroad work greatly exceeded the number of positions available every year. Of course the larger private companies, in metallurgy for example, often had paternalistic pension plans, so the contrast between state-related and private industry is not complete. But here the interesting point is that the unions in these industries never tried to include pension demands in collective bargaining efforts, until the 1936 Matignon agreements stipulated the presence of worker representatives in the administration of pension schemes. The conclusion seems inescapable: distracted by relative indifference of their labor organizations, most workers were able to convert their concern about aging into concrete programs only with outside help, if only because other problems seemed more pressing.

Yet the concern was very real, if not unambiguous; the contrast to the approach of the general labour movement was marked. Here we return to 1911 for two reasons: first, that ordinary workers forced their unions to change their minds about an admittedly meager state plan and second, relatedly, that actual retirement behavior for the bulk of the working class can be dated roughly from this point. It was really pressure from below that forced the CGT to take a mellower stance on pensions after 1910. A gas worker explained his views to the 1911 congress, commenting on the scheme that promised him a pension at 60: 'I'm not sure of reaching this age; but I can say this, that I'm quite content to have the withholding taken because I'm calm about the future.'[38] A widespread realization developed, as at the SFIO congress a year earlier, that masses of workers would turn away from any organization that did not take a constructive stance on the pension question. Of course there was a desire for a better law, one that involved no dues and offered a lower retirement age; but concerned workers seemed to agree that some law was better than none. After the 1910 law passed, the textile federation was assailed by members criticizing the union's opposition, for the workers believed that a more pragmatic approach would have produced an improved system. And, with some exceptions, the workers rushed to sign up for the voluntary plan; by the second trimester of the plan's operation over three million people were subscribed. Some local unions were even asking for higher dues; needless to say, the textile union quickly agreed that participation was permissible pending the next congress discussion.[39]

With the passage of the 1910-11 laws we do reach a potential watershed in the history of older workers in France. Because of workers' pressure the revised 1911 law uniquely provided for retirement at age 60, though one could work longer. Here was concrete result of syndicalist-socialistic rhetoric related in turn to a widespread belief that no one lived this long anyway. But the benefits involved were meager, quite apart from the fact that the plan was voluntary and many younger workers, operating on the class culture which paid no heed to old age as a real possibility, did not enroll. Full benefits, for a new subscriber, would accrue only in 1936, but temporarily the state promised to provide, from those contributions collected plus general tax funds, something like a third of the average laborer's salary upon retirement at age 60 (benefits for widows were half of this sum). This was some gain, however meager. But we stressed above that it all constituted a *potential* watershed, and this qualification deserves exploration now in two respects. First, the outlook of organized labor changed not a whit, nor apparently did grass-roots pressure on it. Second, worker behavior changed mightily, which brought it in possible conflict with labor groups and also, more poignantly, into a situation in which retirement might easily be beyond a worker's control and, once achieved, meaningless or even debilitating.

Again, let us start with the segment more easily documented: what organized labor did. With one or two exceptions the movement had little sense of being goaded as it devoted scant attention to the pension and retirement problem between the world wars. Reformist unions still reported a majority desire to have some pension, but discussion of improvements was limited.[40] All this in a sense confirmed the general working-class approach. Once a pension system was installed it would be defended, but a widespread desire for major innovation was not likely to be forthcoming. The fact that the average worker would now retire was simply not reflected within organized labor.

Several factors produced this ambiguous outlook, and they reflect working-class culture toward aging. First, workers, like their leaders, had many other problems to deal with, material and ideological; this undoubtedly distracted them between the wars. They could not indulge the concern of the minority of state employees, who had a stake in the system if only because they alone were compelled to contribute. Second, young workers still were rarely interested in pension plans at all, because they were costly and remote and because young workers really did not expect to live to retirement. This latter point remains vital, for in contrast to published manuals, gloomy enough, workers did not even expect to drag themselves into senility in the first place. In the upsurge of concern manifest before World War One, it was workers over 55 who took the lead, fearful that blind opposition to the law would deprive them of any benefits. It is not fanciful to suggest that they must have been surprised really to be in need of support for old age. Young workers were uninvolved, and and rarely signed up. This rift continued, for workers' attitude toward old age changed slowly if at all; in the 1930s a number of strikes broke out in the north, fed by younger workers, against the new dues levied for social insurance. The small number of unions with an ongoing concern for pensions often noted that their members were 'trop insouciant' to seek what they needed for their old age.[41]

Furthermore, among blue-collar workers, the pension demands that did develop were directed more toward aiding family members than aiding oneself. Once a minimal pension system was established workers were far more bent on improving benefits to widows and orphans than on increasing their own fund. Miners wanted half pensions for illegitimate as well as legitimate wives and children. Merchant seamen wanted full transferability to widows.[42] For both this group and railway workers frequently commented that they did not expect to live to profit from their pensions. This is why railway workers professed their willingness to pay dues so that pensions would belong 'incontestably' to them and could go to their relatives when they died.[43] Merchant seamen viewed pensions as 'the only means permitting them to provide for their needs and those of their families' once they died.[44] Here again the contrast with white-collar workers was marked, for this class viewed pensions as their own property specifically so that they could retire. In sum, younger workers paid little heed to pensions at all; family men saw them as means to protect the family, drawing perhaps from their experience in seeing wives survive their husbands and not expecting to live past work; as before, only the workers who actually approached retirement could develop an active concern for their own old age, and their voice was rarely strong.

All this made it easy for labor leaders to capitalize on a culture of fatalism. The CGTU, for its part, emphasized the need for attention to youth and continued to blast worker dues and capitalization of pension funds; pensions were not even listed among its specific goals for social legislation. Retirement should be at fifty, for 45 percent of all workers died before reaching that age; radical demography had not changed too much.[45]

The CGT, now reformist rather than revolutionary, spent some time defending the social insurance package proposed by the socialists in 1920 (and enacted in 1930). This included a greatly improved pension scheme, but buried it among provisions for accident, illness, and other disasters — disasters in which the union movement was more interested. Signs of the reformist approach abounded. Dues were now taken as normal; hence, smugly, invocations of how responsible the CGT was in not pandering to worker opposition to contributions, which could be overcome by the realization of resulting advantages. Age of retirement had declined as an issue; the CGT wanted 55 but accepted 60 (65 for white-collar workers). Capitalization could even be defended as much safer than redistribution schemes. But in all this pensions rarely received more than passing mention. Illness, accidents, and unemployment gained most attention.[46] And after the law was passed the federation was content to urge its application to a few new groups of workers and protection for workers who were now growing old but had been unable to pay dues during the decades before the system was established. (As if to prove that no trade union approach in France conduced to much attention to old age, the Catholic union movement echoed its support for the social insurance law and devoted no time at all to its pension provisions.)[47]

Even after World War Two formal discussion of old age was stagnant. Neither the Communist nor the Socialist party mentioned pension problems in their congresses. The textile workers' federation in 1946 noted the problem of keeping pensions up with the cost of living and praised the newly established repartition system as vastly preferable to the 'iniquitous' capitalization procedure; here was one nightmare laid to rest by inflation, for only across-the-board allocation of dues allowed pensions to keep pace with prices. Naturally there was firm, if not very wordy, support for the new social security system which, it was noted, did improve the scale of old age benefits; occasionally more of the same was requested.[48] But this approach was in a sense the apotheosis of letting some other agency take care of the problem; unions and parties could wash their hands of the issue. Small wonder that one observer recently judged that a real interest in aging on the part of French labor dates only from 1971.[49] Until this point it seemed that neither variations nor evolution of ideology produced any real division over the importance of older workers, who were to be commiserated with but largely ignored, even if they caused a few rousing debates over the nature and feasibility of a pension system.

Yet by 1926, if not slightly before, most blue-collar workers were retiring by age 65. Why no major outcry, of the sort that sensitive labor leaders could not ignore, as pensions proved patently inadequate? First, the 1910 voluntary plan provided no easy target, for its results varied with the dues paid; railroad workers or miners, in contrast, under different systems, had specific pension figures to go by, which gave them a focus for attack. Furthermore, by the 1940s at least, older people did not regard material want as their main problem in life, which constituted another disparity between both the government and labor movement approach and the actual needs of the elderly to which we must return. But there is no question that workers could have organized to fight the inadequacy of their pensions after World War One, for inflation steadily eroded the value of their benefits. This is not a political statement or a case of counterfactual history; white-collar workers did precisely this, vigorously, from about 1926 onward. The working class itself, preoccupied with other problems and not really believing in old age, simply let the matter slide. They thought they were old at 45 or 50; therefore the system that existed was irrelevant, save as it provided for widows and orphans. By the time they actually did retire, for their pessimistic self-evaluation was increasingly off the mark, it was too late to worry. Even the lowering of the retirement age to 60, in the 1911 revision of the 1910 law, was really not adequate. Groups of workers such as the merchant marine and railway labor persistently raised the idea of retirement after a certain number of years at work regardless of age (15 and 20, respectively, in the most common proposals) in another variant of this concern. The persistent clash between their concept of aging and that of decision-makers in society at large helps account for the relatively low level of interest in legislative reforms between the wars.[50]

Several factors were involved in the ongoing concept of aging. For public rhetoric the idea that society should arrange free support after a life of nasty and unrewarding toil was doubtless widely believed. If society didn't cough up, to hell with it, pending the revolution.[51] But society's obligation was less compelling than the widespread association of aging with decrepitude. 'Once a man has reached fifty years of age he's reached such a state of exhaustion that he should profit from the work he's produced during his entire life.'[52] 'An immutable principle is that at 50 years a man, and especially a worker, is exhausted; it's at this moment that society should assist him.'[53] Society's obligation really derived from the fact that workers had been 'used up' in its service.[54] The image of exhaustion obviously helps explain why old age was commonly associated with other disasters in a worker's life, such as illness and accidents. Indeed much of the interest in pensions stemmed from an earlier concern for payments to disabled workers. Old age, then, was a period in which one could no longer work — the railway union defined men whose pensions were so low that they had to work beyond the 60-year retirement age as 'broken by age and fatigue.'[55] Exhaustion led inexorably to the theme of decay. The old worker is one 'whose strength has disappeared'[56] — again the importance of a physical definition. And a worker past 60 was not merely old; he was virtually dead. One CGT delegate blasted the notion of retirement at sixty: 'to be able to profit from it one would have to be on the verge of kicking the bucket, and as you know not everyone reaches this age.'[57] While at 65: 'at that age the least infirmities with which they run the risk of being afflicted are paralysis or decay.'[58] Even between the wars, when the retirement age had been set at 60 in the leading plans and proposals, labor representatives could not shake the association between cessation of work and death. A socialist defended his pension plan 'in order that an old person can have his last mouthful of bread before his hour of death.'[59] This image can be traced over virtually the past century; certainly it changed little from the 1890s to the 1940s. Various views were reinforced by an ongoing working-class pessimism, so that each catered to the other. Even new pension laws provided no major breaks in outlook, though they might affect behavior.

Between the wars, however, one new ingredient entered the labor movement approach. Now accompanying the association of exhaustion with middle age was the pervasive desire to yield one's place to a new generation that could handle the work, and here white- and blue-collar unions shared similar attitudes. Labor organizations, once involved in pension plans, pushed this idea assiduously; they typically found their employers in agreement. The postal federation advocated early retirement 'so that there will be more numerous vacancies, not only in the jobs involving promotions but in postmen's jobs, to allow the trainees and laborers to win tenure.'[60] Match workers criticized those of their fellows who resisted retirement, for they blocked the way of others. Hence unions fell easily into the habit of talking of compulsory retirement; the postal workers advocated reduction of pensions for each year worked beyond 55.[61] They admitted that some workers might wish to stay on, but insisted that no one jeopardize 'the rejuvenation of the personnel, which is a necessity.'[62] Obviously this fitted the union's interest in protecting advancement and attracting new members, but it followed also from the denigration of old age. Hence, as the railway union put it, workers should not wish to labor for 'a few pecuniary advantages,' which would only lead them to an early death.[63] Teachers similarly had to be forced out of the classroom; when their union expected compulsory retirement at 55, in 1936, its chairman noted: 'I know that not all who are going to be affected by the decree we anticipate on age limits will welcome the moment when they leave their classroom to accept a retirement which they've nevertheless richly deserved, but we must make room for the young.'[64]

So the idea of age meaning inability to work had to be enforced where necessary. Although manual workers had never initiated retirement schemes their vision of old age allowed them to accept retirement when a pension seemed to assure survival. The association of age with exhaustion had, obviously, a firm empirical base. Yet

worker attitudes and trade union policies offered a few anomalies, at
least by the interwar period. A society that was aging rapidly seemed
most concerned about assuring the advancement of youth. And the
related concept of old age remained static despite the numerical
increase of older people and some incipient improvements in their
health. The fact that some workers seemed to want to cling to their
jobs suggested a partial contradiction between the prevailing culture
and the realities of old age. What workers expected from their old
age and what some of them actually experienced could differ
increasingly. Many must still have been surprised at the very fact
of passing their fiftieth year. Others, surprised or not, resented being
pushed out of a job by employer-union edict. Material wants, given
low pensions, pressed some, but so did self-identification through
work.

For the fact was that those who did live to an older age, and
particularly those who managed to retire, found in working-class
culture only the vaguest hints about what life after retirement would
be like. Most of the images were indirect, for retirement was above all
the cessation of work, the abandonment of jobs that had at best
been strenuous, at worst 'against nature.'[65] Retirement should be a time
of peace and rest. With rare exceptions it was assumed that if a pension
sufficed for material needs, old age should cause no further concern.
Between the wars a few unions worried only lest pensioners encounter
an unsympathetic bureaucracy in collecting their dues. A CGT
delegate had earlier talked of the importance of living honorably, not
vegetating, but he was referring mainly to the need for a satisfactory
pension, which would cover the extra medical attention anticipated.[66]
This approach followed logically from the concept of a broken man
who neither could nor should work any further. It undoubtedly
corresponded with the aspirations of many workers who thought about
retirement at all, for the condition was seen more as ending an
unpleasant experience than beginning a pleasant one.

And here we come to the actual behavior of workers, which can
be described more easily than evaluated. Retirement increased,
rapidly becoming a common phenomenon for the first time in the
history of the class. But with this, and admitting an immense variety
of individual reactions, we return to the potential tragedies prepared
by working-class culture (and expressed widely in the labor movement).
First, of course, inadequate material preparation, so that retirement
was a time of immense physical hardship, quite apart from deterioration
of health. But second, the lack of any active concept of what

retirement should be: it represented stopping something, work, but did it represent starting or continuing anything of interest? Without pretending to fathom the fate of retirees as a whole, for even in old age, and perhaps particularly then, individual variations are immense, we can suggest that a rapidly changing behavior pattern found no correspondence in public policy or collective activities.

There are of course vast difficulties with using the census to project retirement. The 1911 census is virtually worthless because it changed job definitions: the 1921 census was distorted by the aftermath of war, in terms of employment categories. So admitting problems and imprecisions, let us begin with a potentially unusually precise measurement: the work fate of the age cohort (male) 40-44 in 1901 when they had aged 25 years, by 1926. According to mortality figures adjusted for the whole period, 19 percent would have died in this period. Thirty-nine percent were still working (compared to 76 percent among employers, 5 percent among employees; clearly workers were beginning to carve out a notion of retirement closer to the lower middle class than to the proprietary groups). Obviously one can still claim that mortality figures for workers would be unusually high and that the census did not capture part-time work in which the elderly had to engage. But other figures suggest change, beyond the fact that the raw data now indicate a 100 percent increase (from 30 per cent plus to 60 percent plus) in the number of workers retired. Perhaps most striking was the decline in the number of older workers found in totally unskilled jobs: in 1926 only 0.3 percent of all workers over 55, employed in any category, were involved in general labor.[67]

Not surprisingly, given the additional impulse of the depression, the pattern of increased retirement was elaborated in the decade after 1926. Here we take the 55-and-over category for 1926 and compare them to the 65-and-over group for 1936. About 12 percent would have died, given again a pessimistically working-class adjustment to the general mortality figures. Only 22 percent of all male workers and 29 percent of all female workers were still employed. The depression showed its hand in a 223 percent increase of general laborers over 65; on the other hand the 163 percent increase in outright unemployed was below the national level of 370 percent. In neither case were significant absolute numbers of percentages of the elderly involved. Older industrial distinctions still had some bearing. While only 11 percent of all transport workers continued after 65, 20 percent of textile and metallurgical workers did so, and a surprising 37 percent of all printers. But in many trades the principle of retirement, almost invisible at the beginning of the century, had now become dominant: only 14 percent of construction workers persisted, 10 percent of all metal-workers, 6 percent of all wood workers, and so on.[68]

Thus in the quarter century after 1911 retirement became the norm for those older workers who did not die before reaching age 65. By 1946 the revolution seemed complete: only 1 percent of all male and female workers over *60* were employed (compared to 7 percent for the whole population).[69] A life-style that had been imposed on the working class had now become dominant in comparison to virtually every other social group.

For the working class, retirement reached majority proportions by 1926, for those who reached 65; by 1936 the figure had reached over 75 percent for males, so that the post-war phenomenon mainly involved a lowering of age. But what caused this dramatic change in behavior? Above all, was it desired by those involved? These questions, though susceptible to a variety of answers, return us to the odd coincidence between the outlook of workers toward old age and that expressed more formally by worker organizations. The fact that retirement now became common did not change union or party policy immediately, as we have seen. Nor, even for retirees themselves, did it represent a dramatic shift in the view of old age.

For the most obvious cause of the extension of retirement, the existence of a definite if, for most workers, still voluntary pension fund after 1911 must not be exaggerated. Clearly it has a great deal to do with the chronology of the spread of retirement, for some aid was provided to workers, even before their own contributions would entitle them to full pension rights (which again, depending on 25 years of dues paying, was to occur only in 1936). This support may have reduced the need for older people to apply for charity in kind at the *Bureaux de bienfaisance:* between 1922 and 1925 only about 2 percent of the population over 70 were involved in this per year, perhaps because the aid granted now seemed so derisory. Nor was there an increase in those over 70 seeking sickness benefits under the 1905 law; this stayed at roughly 20 percent. Here, however, given the necessity of proving impoverishment plus the fact that the health of the elderly was not deteriorating, persistence is unsurprising.[70] But there was a notable increase in the older people coming into the *hospices,* those dreaded institutions which the poor had feared so long. Again in the early 1920s, the percentage of the elderly population entering a *hospice* began to creep up to 5 percent annually. Authorities explained this by noting that the existence of the pension law called the attention of people to other facilities to which they had rights. It was also true that entrance to a *hospice* became a slightly more rational decision, were the older workers aware of historical trends; though average length of stay altered slightly, at 237 days, the annual death rate had dropped to 17 percent. This suggests some medical advance but also, perhaps, the fact that slightly healthier older people, now forced into retirement, had no other place to go.[71]

For the increase in retirement had causes other than the existence of new facilities, though we cannot quantify their importance. Unskilled jobs diminished in importance: old coachmen and carters, for example, gave way to semi-skilled cabbies and truckers, and this reduced one work recourse for the elderly. Employers, imbued with the new doctrines of efficiency, adopted speed-ups and time and motion studies that left the elderly at a new disadvantage. Before World War One an old worker, unable to work as fast as his younger colleagues, could sometimes make do by working longer, indulging in less absenteeism, and so on.[72] Now, with employers able to disclaim cruelty by pointing to the existence of pension funds, to which they too contributed, could simply fire.[73] Unions played their own role, as they increasingly urged workers to retire to give place for the young. The labor movement's fascination with youth and its promotion made retirement obviously attractive. It is important to note that by the 1930s the labor movement matched this concern with somewhat more regular attention to the material problems of retirement, which increased numbers plus unemployment plus earlier inflation had obviously made acute; the fact that the Matignon agreements, under government guidance, first brought pensions into the collective bargaining areas had something to do with this as well. A new *Fédération des retraités,* formed in the mid-thirties, had active CGT backing. The Federation not only wanted higher pensions but also discussed the psychological problems of retirement, suggesting the construction of workers' retirement homes as an answer, where workers could retain some independence and avoid the deathtrap *hospice.*[74] But this sophistication was superficial, for not a single home was built and the organization admitted that it was still too inexperienced, as well as too poor, to know what retired workers needed and wanted. Hence union policy remained youth-oriented. As a result retirement organizations, most of them admittedly white-collar, shunned involvement with the unions,[75] not only as politically divisive but because of the unions' indifference to their cause. One postal clerk summed up a view that many workers doubtless shared, in noting that most of his colleagues took jobs whenever they could, unless they were really sick, but, able to serve only as replacements, suffered a cut in pay to the benefit of the younger people who had replaced them: 'In reality, to explain this phenomenon of retirement, there is above all the ferocious appetite of the young.'[76]

All of these impulses persisted. Post-war polls showed employers convinced, well beyond reality, that older workers are bad workers and should be pensioned off. Unions continued to talk about the need to make room for promotion. And all this in a labor-short country, with a massively increasing percentage of healthy old people, which in effect chose to import unskilled foreigners rather than devise appropriate methods of work for the old.[77]

Yet quite possibly, in 1911 as in 1946, most older workers really did want to retire. Convinced that old age brought misery, discontented with their work, which undeniably became harder or downgraded with age,[78] retirement may have seemed quite desirable. Surely it did for some, and not just the disabled. We must note the element of compulsion in the new retirement figures, but this does not mean that most workers would have resisted even if they could. What we can assert is that unlike the white-collar group that planned more for retirement and expected to use it to some enjoyment, the working class found nothing new to do with their retired years; their culture had not prepared them to live so long and it did not ready them for innovation once old age was normally capped by cessation of work. Slightly increased institutionalization suggests new strains within the extended family, where there were in any event, given France's declining working-class birth rate, fewer children available to help with support. But older patterns could persist, and one retired railroader pleaded for support for his spinster daughter, who had stayed to take care of him and who should receive the same pension benefits as a wife.[79] Many did in fact keep working, at occasional jobs where they could set their own pace, noting that this not only provided needed money but the only way they found to feel alive; thus a centenarian, a former hat worker, who cut and sold wood in the countryside.[80] The rural motif continued to be important, and the railroad retirement journal was full of advertisements for small cottages with gardens.

All of this indicates that, as before with the minority of retirees, an immense variety prevailed. Bucolic pleasures, family contacts, continued part-time work — a host of combinations might create a pleasant retirement. But there was nothing new enough to match the fact that retirement was now the norm. No associations, with the one exception of the railroaders,[81] sprang up to link retirees within an area to older non-pensioned workers or any aspect of a past occupation, in marked contrast to the proliferation of *Amicales* among retired white-collar workers. And the few publications that purported to represent working-class retirees almost without exception focused strictly on material problems, ignoring the question of what one was supposed to do with one's days once retired. Indeed their whole notion of retirement mirrored the culture of the working-class organizations: with 'life used up' at 65, retirement was at best 'a bit of repose before dying.'[82] Contrast this with the white-collar outlook, which was by no means totally free of this pessimism but which groped toward a sense that retirement might mean something more than vegetation: for one teacher retirement meant 'repose legitimately earned and which gives one the ability to profit from some years of leisure.'[83]

In sum, a massive change in behavior, whether compelled or welcomed or a bit of both, produced little new activity or outlook. There were workers who used traditional means to benefit from retirement or who, individually, even innovated. But the growing gap between a new phenomenon and an unchanged public culture must be emphasized, and it could be tragic. At the very least it produced the odd disparity between organized labor and the problem of retirement between the wars, after the brief upsurge of debate around 1911 — a disparity involving not only pension levels, but also what to do with one's time even if sheer survival was not a problem.

History is crucial to an understanding of present-day working-class culture even if it brings a message of gloom. Cultural persistence is not our only theme, but for the working class the French experience offers evidence of ongoing trends which are at best beginning to be modified. Continuities in the approach of the labor movement remain considerable. Old age has been seen as a purely material concern and somewhat limited even in this regard though the organizational involvement in pension plans is now substantial.[84] Paradoxically, if only because of the left's success in winning a more solid pension program, older workers themselves consistently play down material difficulties in favor of problems of personal adjustment. Relatedly, privately negotiated supplementary pension plans which loom large in the French system add 25 percent to 50 percent to the social security minimum for workers compared to the levels of upper white-collar personnel, whose separate private system expresses not only class advantage but a continuing tradition of greater preparation for retirement.[85] The labor movement has served its older constituents inadequately because of its continuing concern with youth and with an ethic of productive work. Certainly it has missed some important opportunities, in failing to provide the kind of issues that would rouse older workers to a greater political interest; here the protracted inability to recognize the numerical significance and potential of the older population has made an enduring mark. This has left older workers in a curious dilemma. A significant improvement in their lot would require a reordering of society, as radicals long ago recognized; they can expect little attention from the conservative parties. Yet the traditional interests of the left have limited the political response to the problems of aging as well. And the outlets for older workers, which still develop slowly, note the neglect. A periodical in 1957 articulated more clearly concerns evident twenty years before: unions abandon the old, leaving them to impotent groups of their own number despite the role these people played in building the labor movement: the unions stand for youth, and youth too often pushes the old to retire 'without knowing what this means.'

And of course the inattention from labor leaders helps explain the persistence of the more basic cultural traditions. Retired workers even repeat slogans of earlier campaigns over pension law; several in a recent survey characterized their inadequate funds as 'too little to live on, too much to die on' — a phrase first used in 1902.[86] The association between aging and dying has yielded to the somewhat more benign realities of modern senescence, but the theme of exhaustion, and the related need for repose, persists, and again this distinguishes the worker from other elements of society. In 1946 the average French worker retired officially at 58, and almost two-thirds of the class argued for their retirement plans in terms of their diminished physical capacity or their need for rest. The importance of giving way to the young was mentioned repeatedly.[87] At the end of the 1960s over a half of all construction workers sought retirement around sixty (13 percent before 60, 38 percent between 60 and 64); again the 'right to repose' was the most common explanation. Just as revealingly, 66 percent of the actual retirees found themselves in bad health, stressing their loss of physical strength.[88] And before retirement the vast majority insisted that they wanted to do no work after their pension started: 'Once repose is attained, they want complete repose.'[89] Many still saw retirement primarily as the cessation of a job they had disliked, for we must recall that retirement was never a *positive* working-class concept.

All of this may be quite realistic even so. That about twice as many

older workers than functionaries judge their health to be bad reflects
a past of greater stress and a present in which pension levels still differ
markedly by class. But the now-distorting role of working-class culture
cannot be denied. More than other classes, workers fail to think about
retirement save in terms of what they will not be doing; and so many
are disappointed when they actually retire. All recent surveys show a
considerable increase in the number of workers who would like at least
partial jobs, when polled *after* retirement instead of before; this
reflects inadequate pension levels, of course, but also boredom. Among
working-class retirees 'sitting around' heads the list of recreations — a
problem for all classes, to be sure, but enhanced by the persistent
working-class culture.[90] 'Things will be OK as long as I can work, but
after that I can't see very clearly.'[91] This is a theme echoed and
re-echoed, for the most tragic cultural persistence is the failure to
realize that one will actually live to retirement, that all these pension
plans have any personal meaning. 'I never thought of stopping work.
I thought I'd be dead before, I was so tired,' says one disenchanted
pensioner; and another, 'I never thought of stopping at all. I lacked
foresight.'[92] Hence the failure to anticipate activity after the job:
'My days are all the same. . .I get up, I eat, I sleep.'[93] Equally serious
is the question of health, for all observers of the French working class
note that its health now is far superior to its own belief. The 1968
study of construction workers found 55 percent of all men, 51 percent
of all women retirees claiming their health bad or very bad (compared
to less than 40 percent of retired state functionaries). And the belief did
not increase with greater age; that is, a majority of workers judged
themselves in bad health well before retirement and never shook the
view; the minority was equally stubborn in finding their health good —
suggesting again a combination of individual personality, genuine
health differences, but also cultural conditioning. Thus the role
gerontologists increasingly assign to expectations and fears in
magnifying health problems of older people has a particularly
unfortunate impact on the majority of the French working class.[94]

Working-class culture and the continued dependent situation of the
class combine to keep workers rather separate from middle- and
upper-middle-class attitudes towards aging. Unprepared to think too
seriously about retirement until it is upon them and reliant on an
inadequate pension system, workers failed, as we have seen, to develop
the kind of rich complementary funds that functionaries and even
employees established as soon as they were incorporated into the state
system.[95] They are remote from the happiness literature developed for

the middle-class market from the mid-1950s. The happiness literature can be galling, and it does not describe the experience of even middle-class retirees in its impression of a carefree, healthy, sexually stimulating existence until a not-to-be-mentioned event ends the whole process. But it does seek to respond to an increasingly lengthy period of life for which working-class culture remains inadequately prepared.

Obviously the French experience is unusual in several respects. The relatively early retirement age that developed with the maturing of the post-war social security system is given meaning by the fact that in 1968 25 percent less of the post-65 French population was employed than their American counterparts, a difference that relates closely to the pessimistic view of both work and old age that we have seen manifest in virtually every French discussion of the question of retirement.[96] The ideological bent of the French labor movement contributed to a distinctive approach. So did the association of a concern for old age with the advent of much more rapid industrial change around the turn of the century. Workers in most industrialized countries were subjected to an unprecedentedly rigorous pace of work in this period; but where more of them had factory experience already the shock may have been muted. In France the government began considering pensions just as many workers decided they wanted out of the factories as quickly as possible. Something of a durable culture may have resulted, accounting for acceptance of retirement as cessation without positive implication. The fact that France has long had a higher percentage of older people in the population may have had an influence on the working-class view. The unions' concern with making a place for youth might have developed in part because there were so few youth to be found, and the presence of a high percentage of older people exacerbated the concern for making room for new blood — even though in fact competition for place was less severe in France's demographic situation. It is not too far-fetched to suggest that the presence of a large percentage of older people has a depressing effect both on older people themselves and on people contemplating aging — at least in a society where no appropriate culture for aging has developed.[97]

The history of the working-class culture toward aging need not imply immutability. Indeed, one of the purposes of recording the history must be to suggest the need for alternatives, for breaks with an unsatisfactory past. As noted, during the 1950s and 1960s some older French workers began to return to the job, on at least a part-time basis; up to 22 percent of all people over 65 were working by the early 1960s, and among males alone the figures neared 45 percent. The workers divided almost evenly between those who said they were pressed by material need and those who said the job gave them a sense of participating in life which they had lost in a few months of pure retirement. Post-war older workers are much more likely to remain in the city, usually in independent housing which they chose during their prime years.[98] In other words, some new patterns are visible and some reversals to customary forms of behavior, as in the greater interest in work, though perhaps with new reasoning involved. And finally, literally at the beginning of the 1970s, the unions themselves began to develop serious programs dealing with the social needs of the elderly, following from the informal card-playing and reading groups that had sprung up in the post-war years, as retirees groped on their own to find a purpose in life.[99] All of this is tentative still. What the proper range of alternatives for advanced age in the working class should be — how much work, how much association, how much recreational innovation — has yet to be spelled out clearly. Hopefully a serious consideration of a dismal but persistent past may allow old people themselves, and those who have or should have responsibility for improving the framework of their lives, to point up the concerted attention necessary, beyond issues of the mere economics of support for a growing group of elderly, for a proper life in a France where the active worker already outnumbers the older worker by barely two to one.

And a study of the relationship between the French working class and the problem of aging can suggest some important concerns for historians dealing with any industrial society. For experience in France suggests that both the working class and the labor movement developed some important predispositions concerning the aging process quite early, initially on the basis of traditional popular culture and empirical grounds that, if not entirely accurate, at least made considerable sense. It was difficult to envisage old age and, while it might seem desirable to escape work, it was difficult to make positive plans for retirement other than sheer survival. These pre-dispositions did not embellish the actual behavior that developed by the 1920s, that is, the fact of majority retirement, though they may help explain willingness to retire. They give us a tragically profound historical dimension to the problems of retirement, for working-class culture could easily encourage the act but it provided little guidance for what to do after the act. And the apparent persistence of this culture suggests a special role for historical understanding as we belatedly seek to grasp a phenomenon that is in fact basic to modern society.

Notes

1. See, for example, Hugues Destrem, *La Vie après 50 Ans* (Paris, 1966), pp.11ff.
2. Ministère des Affaires Sociales, *Données chiffrées concernant le troisième âge* (Paris, 1969), p.3; Fernand Boverat, *La Vieillissement de la population* (Paris, 1946), pp.16ff.
3. *Statistique générale, Mouvement de la population, 1900* and *passim*; censuses from 1896 to 1911 provide careful analyses of surviving children by class and age. The dearth of surviving children did not persist, as we shall see, but when modified the behavioral patterns of the elderly were already established.
4. Peter Laslett, *The World We Have Lost* (New York, 1965), pp.96ff.
5. J.P.A. Villeneuve-Bargemont, *Economic politique chrétienne* (Paris, 1834), II, p.281.
6. Michael Anderson, 'Family, Household and the Industrial Revolution,' in Peter Laslett (ed.), *Household and Family in Past Time* (Cambridge, 1972). It should be noted that Anderson partially misinterprets his own figures, so far as older workers are concerned. Noting that only 10 percent of his families in Preston were coresidential, he is drawn to comment on the barriers poverty placed on coresidence in most workers' homes – leaving one to wonder what happened to the majority of the aged. Undoubtedly there was resistance to housing the elderly, but the 10 percent figure suggests that most textile workers overcame it. For coresidence would normally be necessary or possible only for a few years, given mortality rates after 55 or so; hence any given census would show only a minority of households as being coresidential even if most elderly workers were so housed. On the limitations on working-class women, see Peter N. Stearns, 'Working-Class Women in Britain, 1890-1914,' in M. Vicinus (ed.), *Suffer and Be Still* (Bloomington, Ind., 1972), pp.100ff.
7. Susanne Pacaud and M.D. Lahalle, *Attitudes, Comportements, Opinions des personnes agées dans le cadre de la famille moderne* (Paris, 1968), p.81. Only 15 percent of those surveyed wanted to live with their children (although a slightly higher fraction did so); 77 percent wanted independent housing and 6 percent preferred an old age home.
8. Fritz Schuman, *Auslese und Anpassung der Arbeiterschaft in der Automobilindustrie* (Leipzig, 1911), *passim*.
9. Fédération francaise des travailleurs du verre, *Congrès national* (Lyons, 1903), p.57.
10. This chapter focuses mainly on men, whereas the history of aging is demographically more female than male. A working-class woman, now marrying relatively early, might also feel that her life crested in her twenties, when she could work, then marry, then bear children. But, so far, we can see older working-class women primarily as filtered through the concerns of their husbands, who were conscious of their need for economic protection but who give us little additional information; or through raw census data, that show the increasing widowhood of all classes so starkly but which must be handled as a partially separate topic.
11. Parti ouvrier, *Septième congrès national* (Paris, 1889), p.14.
12. Confédération générale du travail (CGT), *XVIIe Congrès national corporatif* (Toulouse, 1911), p.278.
13. CGT, *Xe Congrès corporatif* (Rennes, 1898), p.268; see also Fédération française des travailleurs du verre, *Congrès*, pp.57-8.
14. Fédération nationale des travailleurs du bâtiment, *Congrès nationaux,* 1920-1926.
15. Fédération nationale ouvrière de l'industrie textile, *XVIe Congrès national* (Paris, 1920), p.201; CGT, *XIIe Congrès national* (Lyons, 1901), p.137; CGT, *XIe Congrès national* (Le Havre, 1899), p.267.

16. CGT, *IXe Congrès national corporatif* (Toulouse, 1897), p.172.

17. CGT, *XVIIe Congrès, passim.*

18. Parti Socialiste (SFIO), *7e Congrès national* (Paris, 1910), p.303 and *passim.*

19. CGT, *XVIIIe Congrès national corporatif* (Le Havre, 1912), *passim.*

20. CGT, *IXe Congrès,* pp.175ff; *Congrès National des mineurs* (Saint-Etienne, 1892), p.27.

21. It should be clear that while the left can be criticized for their shortsightedness – at least given the fact that the revolution has not come off – they operated in an environment in which the thinking of most of the pension advocates was more retarded still. Hence the parliamentary committee reporting on the pension law in 1897 urged 'a better, wise behavior, more orderliness, more economy' in invoking self-help as the solution to the problem of aging. 'Foresight is a social fact of the greatest importance. It is the act which essentially characterizes the civilized being and distinguishes him from primitive man.' Hence a voluntary pension scheme in which workers and employers would contribute equally, with a tiny state subsidy, to provide a pension at best 10 percent of the average unskilled worker's wage. Chambre des deputés, *Rapport fait au nom de la commission d'assurance et de prévoyance sociales* (#2185, Paris, 1897), pp.3, 5, and *passim.*

22. 'The more miserable a worker is during his life, the more the new tax (the pension dues) burdens him, the more awful his means of existence, the more fearsome his conditions of work, the more he'll be robbed because he'll be dead.' SFIO, *7e Congrès,* p.169.

23. Ministère du commerce, Office du travail, *Les Caisses patronales des retraites des établissements industriels* (Paris, 1898), *passim.*

24. I cannot forebear from citing Professor E.T. Gargan's comment on my book, *Revolutionary Syndicalism and French Labor* (New Brunswick, 1971), in which among the various denunciations of the idea that a worker could be moderate, other than by sheer repression, it was claimed that miners and others were incapable of work after age 45. *Journal of Modern History* (1972), p.436.

25. For an example, Edouard Dolléans, *Histoire du mouvement ouvrier* (Paris, 1953), I, p.21 and *passim.*

26. *Statistique générale de la France, Mouvement de la population,* 1900 and *passim.*

27. Ministère du commerce, *Recensement général de la population,* 1901, 1906, 1911.

28. Michael Marrus, 'Social Drinking in the "Belle Epoque",' *Journal of Social History* (1974), pp.115-41.

29. For these the related statistics, see *Statistique générale de la France, Institutions d'assistance publiques,* 1899ff (before 1899, sparser but useful figures were included in the *Mouvement général de la population).*

30. Even the new law involved, deliberately, a great deal of personal and deterrent indignity; to benefit one had to be 'deprived of resources,' write the local communal aid bureau which listed those who applied and of course decided, often arbitrarily, on the results of the application, their decisions subject to the scrutiny of the municipal council. If one actually applied, however, one often received aid even if not destitute, in that irony of welfare which still lingers, and not only in France: if one admits failure and a certain lack of self-respect (this latter of course depending on personal as well as social definition) one need not necessarily have totally failed or be unrespectable. But admitting that there was much here that involved the eye of the beholder, the aged at first were unaware of their rights or deterred by the conditions or the sheer nuisance involved. Edouard Cheval, *Les Résultats pratiques de la*

loi du 14 juillet 1905 sur l'assistance obligatoire aux vieillards (Chambery, 1911).

31. Michael Anderson, *Family Structure in Nineteenth Century Lancashire* (Cambridge, 1973), *passim;* see chapter IV for more specific French patterns.

32. Pacaud and Lahalle, *Attitudes, passim.*

33. *Statistique générale de la France, Recensement de 1891, passim.*

34. See the censuses from 1896 onward; further study is presented in a later chapter. Already, however, a few dramatic examples: the 1901-1906 censuses in Haute-Savoie reveal an increase in the number of women over 70, obviously impossible due to normal demography. What seems to have occurred was a return (numerically rather small) of life-long servants from Paris and Lyons, which the area had long supplied – presumably with some pension or savings, but possibly with local family support as well. For males, departments like the Eure, while not showing absolute increases, demonstrate far less than normal decreases, suggesting a rural movement out of Paris after 65, and while some of this was middle-class, individual cases were definitely working-class – nominal tracing involves professions like butcher, railroader and so on. This material derives from the manuscript census of the Eure and from interviews with retirees in the village of Dangu.

35. *Congrès du Syndicat national des instituteurs et institutrices publics* (Paris, 1923), p.6; see also *L'Ecole Libératrice,* 28 August 1937.

36. Syndicat national des agents des postes, télégraphes et téléphones, *8e Congrès* (Rennes, 1926), p.363 and *7e Congrès* (Epernay, 1925), p.50; Alliance nationale contre la dépopulation, *Trois journées pour l'étude scientifique du vieillissement de la population* (Paris, 1948), I, pp.85ff.

37. Fédération nationale des travailleurs du sous-sol, *35e Congrès* (Paris, 1921), p.66, Fédération nationale de l'industrie des mines, minières, et carrières, *Congrès national* (Saint-Etienne, 1891); Fédération nationale des travailleurs réunis de la Marine de l'Etat, *2me Congrès* (Toulon, 1905), pp.15, 57; Syndicat national des travailleurs des chemins de fer, *Commentaires de principales revendications* (Paris, 1896), p.14; Fédération nationale de l'éclairage et des forces motrices, *Rapports moral et financier* (Versailles, 1924), pp.13, 14; Fédération nationale des ouvriers et ouvrières des manufactures des tabacs en France, *3me Congrès* (Paris, 1894), p.48; Fédération nationale des ouvriers et ouvrières des manufactures d'allumettes en France, *3e Congrès national* (Marseilles, 1896), p.72.

38. CGT, *XVII Congrès,* p.265.

39. SFIO, *7e Congrès,* pp.170ff, 314; *Compte-rendu du XIIme Congrès national des ouvriers de l'industrie textile* (Lille, 1912), pp.73ff.

40. Fédération unitaire des travailleurs du livre, *2e Congrès national* (Paris, 1925), p.455; Fédération de l'industrie des travailleurs de l'habillement, *XIIe Congrès national de la Fédération* (Lille, 1921), p.61; Fédération nationale des ouvriers de l'industrie textile de France, *XVIIe Congrès national* (Paris, 1922), p.61.

41. Fédération nationale des syndicats maritimes, *Dixième Congrès* (Marseilles, 1902), p.53. Fédération des travailleurs du bâtiment, *XXVIe Congrès national fédératif* (Paris, 1946), p.223; *Compte rendu. . .des ouvriers de l'industrie textile,* pp.73ff; Fédération nationale des travailleurs des P.T.T., *6e Congrès* (Paris, 1932), *passim.*

42. Fédération nationale de l'industrie des mines, minières, et carrières, *Congrès national* (Carmaux, 1910), p.25; Fédération nationale des travailleurs réunis de la marine de l'Etat, *3me Congrès* (Toulon, 1905), p.16.

43. Syndicat national des travailleurs des chemins de fer, *Commentaires,* p.12.

44. Fédération nationale des syndicats maritimes, *Dixième Congrès national* (Marseilles, 1902), p.47.

45. Confédération générale du travail unifié, (CGTU), *Congrès national ordinaire*

(Paris, 1931), p.532; CGTU, *Congrès national ordinaire* (Paris, 1927), pp.370ff.

46. Fédération des ouvriers de métaux, *VIe Congrès fédéral* (Versailles, 1921), pp.115ff; Fédération nationale des syndicats confédérés des travailleurs de l'alimentation, *XIVe Congrès fédéral* (Versailles, 1931), p.56; Fédération nationale des travailleurs du sous-sol, *35e Congrès national* (Paris, 1921), p.66.

47. Confédération française des travailleurs chrétiens, *Circulaire mensuelle,* 31 May 1920ff.

48. Fédération des travailleurs du textile, *XXVIe Congrès national fédératif* (Paris, 1946); CGT, *XXVIIe Congrès confédéral, Rapports confédéraux* (Paris, 1948), p.302; For a survey of the French pension system and its history, 'Le Monde contemporain,' *Les Institutions sociales de la France* (Paris, 1955), pp.35ff.

49. Maurice Guillon, *Les Secrets de la retraite heureuse* (Paris, 1971), p.307.

50. CGT, *XIIe Congrès,* pp.124ff; Fédération nationale des syndicats maritimes, *Douzième congrès* (Marseilles, 1905), p.71; Fédération nationale des ouviers et ouvrières des manufactures des tabacs en France, *3me Congrès,* p.45.

51. CGT, *Congrès confédéral de Paris* (Paris, 1927), p.215; CGT, *Congrès confédéral de Paris* (Paris, 1931), p.137; Fédération nationale des travailleurs des postes, télégraphes, et téléphones, *IIe Congrès* (Limoges, 1922), p.141.

52. CGT, *XVIIe Congrès,* p.279, statement by a delegate from the railway workers.

53. CGT, *XXIe Congrès,* p.143.

54. CGTU Fédération nationale unitaire des travailleurs du sous-sol, *Compte-rendu officiel des travaux de 3me Congrès* (Montceau, 1924), p.94.

55. Syndicat national des travailleurs des chemins de fer, *Commentaires,* p.16.

56. Ibid., p.9.

57. CGT, *IXe Congrès,* p.175.

58. Fédération nationale des ouvriers et ouvières des manufactures des tabacs, *2me Congrès* (Paris, 1892), p.99.

59. SFIO, *XVIIe Congrès national* (Paris, 1929), p.359.

60. Fédération postale confedérée, *14e Congrès national* (Paris, 1928).

61. Fédération nationale des ouvriers et ouvrières des manufactures d'allumettes en France, *3e Congrès,* p.72; Fédération nationale des travailleurs des postes, télégraphes, et téléphones, *IIe Congrès* (Limoges, 1922), p.137.

62. Syndicat national des agents des postes, télégraphes, et téléphones, *9e Congrès* (Rennes, 1927), p.218.

63. Fédération nationale des travailleurs des chemins de fer, *IIe Congrès fédéral* (Paris, 1934), p.129; for a similar opinion even before World War One, CGT, *XIIe Congrès,* p.132.

64. *L'Ecole libératrice,* 19 September 1936, p.1165.

65. Syndicat national des travailleurs des chemins de fer, *Commentaires,* p.8.

66. CGT, *XIIe Congrès,* p.188 and *Congrès confédéral* (1931), p.452.

67. *Recensements généraux de la population,* 1901 and 1926.

68. *Recensements généraux de la population,* 1926 and 1936.

69. *Recensements général de la population,* 1926; Boverat, *Vieillissement, passim.*

70. *Le Mutilé des Ans,* 1937.

71. *Statistique générale de la France, Institutions d'assistance publique,* 1921ff.

72. Peter N. Stearns, *Lives of Labour* (London, 1975), *passim.*

73. Les Etablissements Schneider, *Les Retraites pour la vieillesse* (Paris, 1912); Alliance nationale contre la dépopulation, *Trois journées, passim.*

74. *Tribune des fonctionnaires,* 1936-7; the CGT also supported the journal, *Mutilé des ans,* which began in 1931.

75. *Défense des retraités des chemins de fer,* 1937.

76. *Cri du retraité*, 1930. A worker similarly noted a desire for obligatory pensions detached from the necessity of quitting work. *Mutilé des ans,* 1936.
77. Alliance nationale contre la dépopulation, *Trois journées, passim.*
78. Stearns, *Lives, passim.*
79. *Défense des retraités des chemins de fer,* 1937.
80. *Mutilé des ans,* 1936.
81. *La Femme affranchie* did report in 1930 an association of older non-pensioned workers.
82. *Mutilé des ans,* 1936.
83. E. Devinant, *La Retraite des instituteurs* (Paris, 1907), p.28.
84. For a general summary see Max Horlick and A.M. Skolnik, *Private Pension Plans in West Germany and France* (Washington, 1971), *passim.*
85. *La Vieillesse heureuse,* 1957.
86. Caisse nationale de retraite des ouvriers du bâtiment et des travaux publics, *Réalités du troisième âge: Enquête sur les ouvriers retraités du bâtiment et des travaux publics* (Paris, 1968), p.220.
87. Alliance nationale contre la dépopulation, *Trois journées,* I, pp.85ff; Jean Daric, *Vieillissement de la population et prolongation de la vie active* (Paris, 1948), p.61. It should be noted that the tendency toward early retirement costs mightily in subsequent pension benefits, which reinforces the significance of the felt need. Le Monde contemporaine, *Institutions,* III, pp.35ff.
88. Caisse nationale de retraite des ouvriers du bâtiment et des travaux publics, *Réalités,* pp.16ff.
89. Alliance nationale contre la dépopulation, *Trois journées,* I, p.91.
90. Stearns, *Lives,* chapter VIII; Centre international de gérontologie sociale, *Loisirs et 3e Âge* (Paris, 1972), pp.13ff.
91. Caisse nationale de retraite des ouvriers du bâtiment des travaux publics, *Réalités,* p.88.
92. Anne Lauran, *L'Age scandaleux* (Paris, 1971), pp.49ff.
93. *Idem.*
94. Caisse nationale de retraite des ouviers du bâtiment de des travaux publics, *Réalités,* pp.21ff; Destrem, *Vie,* p.18.
95. Horlick and Skolnick, *Private Plans, passim.*
96. Centre international de gérontologie sociale, *Loisirs,* p.13.
97. Again one must note the long belief that French employers preferred young blood, ignoring the qualities of older workers including high production levels actually attained via fewer accidents, and less absenteeism, despite the French demographic context – or perhaps because of its unusually rapid aging. Alliance nationale contre la dépopulation, *Troix journées,* I, *passim.*
98. Pataud and Lahalle, *Attitudes, passim;* Centre international de gérontologie sociale, *Loisirs,* pp.13ff.
99. This is noted without much elaboration in Guillon, *Secrets,* p.307; see also, though it is not primarily directed toward the working class, the periodical *Trosième Age* about 1968ff.

3 GERIATRIC MEDICINE

The link between medicine and old people has come to be intimate. This section traces what are for all intents and purposes the origins of this link and its evolution. Old people in the nineteenth century rarely saw doctors; they might if they were very rich or if they were very poor and desperately ill. The in-between sector, in terms of income and health conditions, largely stayed away. Old people, in France as in other countries, by 1950 were seeing doctors with increasing regularity and expecting new things from them. This is the basic process that has to be explained.

Yet we cannot leave the topic with this introduction alone, or at least the introduction must be phrased in a more complex manner. The social history of medicine involves three fundamental layers, the first two admittedly not always easy to distinguish. Layer one is the research physician who may (and through most of the nineteenth century normally would) care for ordinary patients but who views his role as contributing new knowledge as well. Layer two is the practicing physician pure and simple (sometimes quite simple). He is hard to capture, but occasional pamphlets and the medical journals give some insight into his outlook and practices (so, in principle, would further work on the training of doctors in France which was fantastically varied, from the animist school of Montpellier which looked for the essential human spirit to the cadaver cutters in Paris, but we touch on this only as it affected specific education in geriatrics). In combination, the sources give a fairly decent idea of what ordinary doctors did with older patients and how their practices have evolved. Layer three, obviously, is the patient himself. Despite the label, we need not regard patients as patient; they can be active agents in medical change. This is what ultimately occurred in the geriatric field, though very recently — after comparable pressure from below in women's medicine, pediatrics and so on. Ultimately, for the human history of geriatrics, we need the entire cake, all three layers, for our social palette.

But for our first section, which runs from the late eighteenth century well into the twentieth, there was no cake. Indeed an appropriate geriatric dessert has yet to be produced, but there has been undeniable progress, whether one prefers a gastronomic or an artistic image.[1]

Geriatrics was born in the nineteenth century; we will establish its credentials in a moment. But it was born at the research level, not abstracted from contact with real people but with little initial relevance to them. It was really part of a cultural evolution, the very evolution we have discussed earlier. That is, it shared traditional assumptions about old people and, even more important, furthered these assumptions by what constituted major landmarks in medical achievement. This is one vital area where the outlook we have described overall colored a field of vital importance to old people. From the standpoint of old people themselves this means three things, which must be retained even as we briefly dive into the most formal medical dicta. First, there wasn't much point going to doctors for they had little to offer, even though their knowledge expanded immensely. Second, the sources of improvement in the medical care of old people would commonly come outside geriatric medicine *per se*. They came from biology, for biologists took quite a different view of old age than most doctors did, and (although less in France, save by imitation, than in other countries) branches of medicine not solely applied to the elderly, such as cardiology. Third, at least until the late 1930s, the health of the elderly depended very little on the state of geriatric knowledge.

And although this is not our primary focus for the nineteenth century, the contentions raise some fascinating questions about what was being done to and by the elderly. What did those doctors who had older patients judge suitable therapy? What did older people do in addition to or instead of seeing doctors? We have some hints, if not a full picture.

We can begin with the predictable contrast, juxtaposing statistics, though meager, with research focus, quite ample. Figures on death causes were offered to the government only in 1859-60; thereafter doctors, even in centralized France, refused to cooperate until the 1920s. In the recorded early years, 5 percent of all males (these data refer to people designated as over 60) died from hypertrophy of the heart; 12 percent from pneumonia, 6 percent from phthisis (or 18 percent from all respiratory diseases) 21 percent from apoplexy, 3 percent from cancer, 2 percent from suicide. Liver disease, kidney disease, but above all 'unrecorded' fill out the desirable 100 percent ('unrecorded'constituted 41 percent). The unrecordeds seem to confirm the point that few elderly had contact with doctors in the nineteenth century, even after death. But those who did, with varying degrees of rigor and with due allowance for changes in

terminology and diagnosis, died of diseases disproportionately unstudied
in the geriatric medicine of the time. Unstudied, or abandoned
as hopeless. The latter applies to respiratory deaths, the former to
heart disease. Cancer was noted but not understood, much less treated.
Only liver, and possibly kidney, disease and apoplexy received
attention from the research doctors. Added up, these causes of death
though important, fell so far short of the ordinary person's experience,
save *in extremis* through apoplexy, that medical consultation made
little sense. And correspondingly the researchers were refining their
knowledge of organic disarray which only a minority of older
people suffered. Bluntly put, the typical researcher opened the
cadaver of someone dead of pneumonia and discovered degenerated
organs; his resulting opus, while possibly recognizing pneumonia as
a killer, centered on the organs, which were neatly, almost
Cartesianly, definable. And thus undeniable advance in geriatric
knowledge in the nineteenth century bore no relationship to adult
longevity rates, which improved somewhat between 1806 and 1809
and 1855 and 1859 (11.7 years at age 60 for males to 12.8 years)
and then dipped so that by 1895 the rate was down to 11.5 years.
Doctors were simply not in control of the situation, and while they
might blame the growth of cities for their impotence it was in fact
the countryside that held the rate roughly constant. And doctors,
while praising the countryside, rarely practiced there.

But having offered a vague statistical profile of the disjuncture
between medicine and geriatric health, we must begin in greater
detail with what can be called the cultural history of medicine, the
outlook and research approach of doctors dealing with geriatrics. This
is obviously the easiest section of our trilogy to handle, even without
great scientific detail, for research physicians were articulate and
wrote for posterity. The development of French geriatric research,
pioneering for many decades, is an indication of the self-fulfilling
power of cultural images. Already in the first chapter we liberally
cited Reveillé-Parise, a leading doctor at the Salpetrière; his book was
more a moral manual than a medical treatise, but it clearly indicates
the overlap between even sophisticated researchers and popular
advice-mongers. Indeed his colleagues tended to look down a bit on
his book because it included wisps of Ciceronian optimism along
with the more approved pathological pessimism. But Reveillé-Parise
could not shake more agonizing classical canons and his own medical
experience largely confirmed them. So we dwell a bit on the
nineteenth-century geriatric pioneer in his own orbit, carefully

recognizing that this orbit affected a very small percentage of actual older people.

The power of a set of attitudes is illustrated here again: if you start pessimistically you likely do research that confirms your pessimism — though it may well be correct. This section has a happier, if not necessarily more realistic, ending than that on worker culture, but the joy was painfully and incompletely won. Doctors are still influenced by the traditions, classical and nineteenth-century, of what the aged are biologically. They have changed largely because of the impulse of non-medical scientists and oddballs within their own profession, *plus* the pressure from patients themselves, mainly from the middle class. In this sense doctors differed from trade union leaders, in that they had an outside pressure (biological science) and a clientele less convinced they were near-dead at 60. But the difference cannot be stretched too far, for doctors only recently converted to a more optimistic approach and that only partially, and many tacitly agree with the general culture that old people are best forgotten until buried save for minimal material care.

From the 1860s, when statistics become available, approximately 2.1 percent of the elderly population over 75 were annually in the *hospices* reserved for old people. One could get in a bit earlier if extremely ill, and the *hospices* also harbored disabled of all ages and incurable children. So we begin with an incorrectable statistical distortion. But the old constituted the vast majority of the *hospice* population, over 85 percent when figures were broken down later in the nineteenth century. Their average stay was 260-300 days a year; only 35 percent left in any given year; and 20 percent died there each year. Putting all this together, it can be calculated that no more than 11 percent of France's elderly ever went to the *hospice* even assuming, unrealistically, no repeat visits.

Two major points emerge from this. First, contrary to widespread impression, the bulk of the elderly were *never* institutionalized with the advent of increasingly modern society. It is true that Paris had slightly higher rates of institutionalization than the rest of France, but this was partly because its hospitals were better-run and provincial doctors sent tough cases there. The elderly shunned institutions and they had enough private or familial backing to manage.

Point two, however, is crucial for our initial analysis: the *hospice* constituted the main contact between the research doctor and the elderly patient. Obviously an incalculable number of wealthier people

saw private doctors. As early as 1800 enough reports were being issued
on method of alleviating bladder blockage, mainly by use of wax
devices, to suggest that many men were accepting treatment for this
common problem. Some menopausal women accepted treatment, though
doctors noted resistance to the most common remedies offered: bleeding,
as well as of course sensible exercise, diet, etc. Men with gout consulted
doctors. But impressionistically this does not add up to a long list of
patients and, as we will see, most researchers drew their generalizations
about the health of the elderly from the non-wealthy minority who
entered hospitals.

Adding to this, finally, is the absence of wide-selling medical
literature designed for the elderly. Pamphlets there were, but they
found no massive market if they were specifically medical. This is in
marked contrast with material written in obstetrics, for example;
doctors had little to say to old people and old people found no reason
to listen — just as the bulk of them shunned the special hospitals
designated for them as death traps. Only after 1920 are there signs
that medical columns designated for the elderly, pamphlets written
for them by doctors, and so on, were having any impact. Until then,
the elderly and the doctors did not mix in any massive fashion. Care
for the elderly was self-procured, often from charlatans, or was the
responsibility of the extended family, using what folk remedies
seemed appropriate.

Yet despite the substantial non-existence of patients, geriatrics was
well launched without them. And here is a vital factor ultimately
affecting old people as well as medical research. French medicine
followed the beat of its own drum in geriatric probings. The research
tier had its own causation, the motivation of one research
development feeding another. Immensely important discoveries
were made, and French geriatrics could long claim a world lead. The
term itself was not coined until the early twentieth century (and in
America), but a word 'gérocomie' was used in 1807 to denote
specialization in the diseases of old people; by the 1830s every major
medical treatise for teaching purposes, at least in Paris, had a section
on the special diseases of the old; and doctors were eloquently
pleading for increased specialization that would deal with old age
as a distinct period of life demanding distinct research and
therapeutics.[2]

Yet again, the sharp gap between interest and practice: between
1817 and 1830 a French person aged 50 could expect 19.9 more years
of life; in 1900, 19.8.[3] This is not a distinctively French problem,

though the deterioration was unusual; only in Holland and the
Scandinavian countries was there consistent improvement in adult
longevity. And we cannot pretend that the nation is an ideal unit for
analysis of geriatrics; French doctors freely cited English and German
works and, later, Italian, Russian and American, although it is
important to note that their borrowing was selective to fit what
became a French medical culture regarding the elderly. And of course,
pace the Dutch and Nordics, one could argue that medicine
heroically maintained adult lifespans despite urbanization and attendant
ill effects of industrialization. This rings a bit hollow for France, save
in mining areas, because urbanization was not concentrated (Paris must
be excluded because longevity improved there), but it constitutes
a possible medical exculpation. Yet the fact remains that research
advance had no visible impact on health. Indeed we will argue, in
connection with the general traditional French culture toward aging,
that medical developments contributed to the association of age with
inherent debilitation and contributes still to the durable hypochondria
among more than half of all French retirees.[4] We must, again, begin
probing this enigma at the research level.

Until after 1870 research, along with eloquent pleas for a
'médecine des vieillards' as a special branch of training and treatment,
emanated almost entirely from the great hospitals designed for the
indigent infirm, incurable, and elderly. The Bicêtre for men, even more
the Salpetrière for women, produced an abundant field for research.
But, as too few doctors noted,[5] the research was on atypical subjects.
As the mortality and departure figures suggest, treatment was not an
active possibility, particularly in the case of women. Statistics show
indigent women much more reluctant than men to enter regular
hospitals in their adult years, by almost 2 to 1, but just as likely to
enter after age 70 by the end of the century, and for longer than
median stays, suggesting illness even more serious than average that
drove them in despite greater family attachment and reluctance to deal
with impersonal institutions;[6] and yet the Salpetrière was the greatest
single center of geriatric research, at least through the famous work
of Charcot in the 1860s and 1870s. Small wonder that the first line
of analysis was pathological, through case studies and autopsies, given
subjects almost surely incurable and, being poor, often female and,
above all, always old, open to any manipulative feelings a researcher
might have in any event. Only a poor second dealt with diagnosis
and symptoms and the poorer third, important in its negative
conclusions but minor in the attention it received — at best relegated

to a small final section in any geriatric treatise until after 1900 —
devoted to treatment.[7]

At the risk of the admittedly anachronistic approach of judging by
what we now know to work, the nineteenth century got off to a good
start in France, before the rapid progress of geriatric pathology — that is,
until the later 1830s. With some borrowings from across the Channel,
semi-surgical procedures to deal with bladder and prostate problems,
mainly in the French case using thin wax sticks, could alleviate one of
the typical and serious complaints of old men. The interest here
reflected legitimate but ultimately excessive concern with facilitating
the elimination of wastes, and certainly few elderly had access to the
new methods; but a considerable body of experience was built up
and enough old men appealed for help to allow the development of
some surgical charlatanage, perhaps a good test of professional arrival,
where doctors, finding their normal route blocked, drained the bladder
blindly, allowing temporary alleviation and related improvement in
reputation at the risk of later infection and hemorrhage in the patient.[8]
The French were also active in labeling diseases such as gout
according to subtypes after the Linnean tradition and in applying the
distinctions in symptoms not only to the rich but to the poor
women in the Salpetrière,[9] in other words adapting concerns
common among those who could afford private practitioners to a
broader population. For gout and diseases other than urinary blockage
there remained little therapy to recommend save the traditional
maxims of moderation, copied faithfully from the classics: care in sex,
drink and food, particularly meat, restrained but regular exercise,
friction massages — these would be endlessly urged by doctors, for lack
of much else to say, into the 1940s,[10] with Galen and Hippocrates but
also Cicero freely invoked. Conceptually the most interesting,
potentially the most promising development was the very recognition of
the elderly as a special health category.[11] Doctors were urged, though
almost surely with little effect, to adapt their treatment to the age of
the patient. It was noted that many old people could not survive
treatments common for adults. Here was an avenue that was ultimately
of great significance as doctors in special contact with the elderly,
especially at institutions like the Salpetrière, pleaded with their
colleagues not to yield to the impulse of applying remedies more
drastically to the old simply because their diseases had more obviously
dangerous implications. It was stressed that the organs of old people
had become worn and atrophied. Normally the stomach and heart
were exempted from this (later the heart and kidney) but aside from

these errors — and it was recognized that in a few cases an old heart might rupture — the general principle was sound if applied to therapeutics. Comments about the degenerated arterial system, blocked by calcification or cholesterol particles, can indeed seem quite modern. The specialists also pointed to the difficulty of diagnosing diseases among the elderly, notably pneumonia, that had far more dramatic symptoms with adults. Lack of fever and the ability to walk and act normally until a sudden crisis gave rise to much anguished comment at the Salpetrière.

Finally, in a renewed plea for the specialization in medicine for the elderly, Dr Prus in the late 1830s sounded a note that was occasionally repeated if not seriously taken up thereafter, but it came from the heart. With adults, even with children, doctors could concentrate on furthering nature's processes. With old people nature had to be fought for nature had now become destructive. How the combat was to be waged Prus did not know, but he urged that it be joined.[12]

A generation later, by 1860, despite great attention to what we would call geriatrics, few advances had been made in potential diagnosis and particularly treatment. Actual practitioners were delighted with the use of the stethoscope but its application to old people was admitted to be limited by the greater percussion even of normal chests. So although the chest was the centre of at least the second most common killer of old people, pneumonia, diagnosis remained tentative. Among the several reasons for the pathological emphasis was this general diagnostic problem, along with the truly agonizing inability to offer novel or effective treatment; it was simplest to analyze the condition after death. Charcot was correct in pointing out that one diagnostic problem was more apparent than real; fever, although not present at the peripheries as with adults, could normally be detected in cases of disease through use of a rectal thermometer. He introduced regular rectal temperature-taking at the Salpetrière in 1863, copying earlier German practice. But his finding was incorporated in a general treatise only in 1904, and his own main emphasis was on pathology, to such an extent that he encouraged several needless errors in diagnosis.[13] Overall, more care was taken, by the warders of the Salpetrière, to chart symptoms and then relate them to detailed findings in autopsies, than even to record the results of various efforts at treatment. Statistics were scrupulously gathered on incidence of hypertrophy of the heart; calcification of the aorta; softening of the brain and its visual and tactile results after death, and so on. All very useful, but no such statistical care was taken in linking remedies with effects. Durand-Fardel, who produced the first general treatise on diseases of the elderly in 1854, one which stood for fifty years, offered figure after figure on post-mortem characteristics, based mainly on several score cases in his practice at the Salpetrière in the 1830s – for obviously even a zealous pathologist could dissect only so much when he had other duties – and to a lesser extent on pre-mortem symptoms and correlations with incidence of death of such factors as season and even time of day. But while the treatment applied might be briefly described, its relation to cures was with one exception entirely ignored. The exception reveals something of the agonizing therapeutic problem as well as the general statistical approach. In discussing pneumonia, 'the most fearsome scourge of old age,' Durand-Fardel tried to establish the death rates; carefully linked incidence with seasons at the Salpetrière (winter and spring were the villains) and with location in the hospital itself (some areas were damper than others); disputed some commonly held beliefs about the symptoms of pneumonia in the elderly, noting that hysteria was not inevitable but occurred in only 18 of 50 cases he had; and then turned to treatment, observing how discouraged doctors at the Salpetrière and Bicêtre became over their ineffectiveness but claiming that impotence was not complete. In order, except when pneumonia followed a stroke or an accident, patients should be bled (if the stethoscope revealed a normal heart), given emetics to encourage spit, antimonials to stimulate vomit or defecation and thus purge the system, and then have vesicatories applied. And finally the lone test of results. In 27 cases where emetics were administered 20 patients died, 7 lived, leading Durand-Fardel to recommend, with no clear logic, a middle-level dosage.[14]

The basic assumptions remained constant even after 1870, when French geriatric research became less imaginative even on the pathological level. In the eighteenth century old age was held to be an adequate explanation for serious disease; as Létienne said, 'a very sufficient reason for decay and disorders.' This concept was, as the general culture already suggested, particularly applied to women. Goubelly, writing in 1785, noted menopause as a critical time, particularly for urban women, judging hysteria and cancer extremely common, both the results of the reflux of humors that could no longer escape through menstruation. Women would be sick from menopause until death, though he charitably noted that they might not die immediately.[15] Views of this sort had an amazing persistence, yet briefly, around 1800, they seemed susceptible to modification. One of the first conceptual achievements of doctors who paid special attention to the elderly was to qualify the idea of the sudden, drastic onset of old age, the 'coup de vieux.' This notion, derived from the Greeks and deeply ingrained in popular belief, divided life into stages, with the healthy adult, as we have seen, dramatically changing into a wrinkled, gray, bald, diseased individual — diseased by the very fact of his age. As early as the first empire Bichat and others were noting the gradual character of aging and, to a lesser extent, its varying rate from one individual to the next.[16] Furthermore, death normally occurred not because of old age itself but because of specific illnesses and malfunctions which could be studied.[17]

If the diseases first examined were rather predictable, such as gout,[18] the discussions of anatomy and symptoms progressively became more complex. Landré-Beauvais introduced a vital change in the approach to brain disorders, through his discoveries in autopsies: softening of the brain was not a fever but senile destruction, rather like gangrene.[19] Durand-Fardel, articulating the common approach, emphasized lesions in the key organic centers — lungs, brain, and vascular system — and offered immense detail on the anatomical changes found after brain hemorrhage, pneumonia and so on. He prided himself, with some justice, as offering the first geriatric manual based on rigorous observation, as opposed to those of Day and Canstatt, observation being in the first instance pathological. He could thus insist on the importance of distinguishing between brain hemorrhage and softening and between both and apoplexy (though this latter distinction was later found fairly useless). He could stress, more prosaically but perhaps just as helpfully in terms of normal practice, the difference between apoplexy and drunkenness.

There were obvious problems with the organic emphasis, of course, for in fact it brought doctors right back to the notion that old age itself was an illness. Diversion of attention from disease to lesions, though not complete, was over-simple, if only because a virtual plurality of old people died directly from respiratory illness (which Durand-Fardel found a normal state in the elderly even if it turned into emphysema). Charcot and others claimed that individual organs could decay singly in the elderly, without causing alterations elsewhere in the system or overt symptoms, an extreme as well as erroneous statement of the pathologist's glee at isolating lesions and one which wasted a great deal of time in debate. There were some odd blind spots in the organic approach itself, as the kidney and heart were normally exempted from the general process of senile atrophy. Cancer was noted but not given great attention, partly because it could not be cured,

partly perhaps because it was less common than now, but partly
because it did not fit neatly into predictable patterns of organic decay.
But important new knowledge developed, including some sense of the
incidence of fatal causes of death among the elderly: lung problems
first, then nervous system and brain, then circulation, then digestive
(including cancer).

And the organic approach could be linked to a much more precise
diagnosis of symptoms. Charcot and others might delight in finding
atrophied organs that had not produced clear symptoms until death
occurred, because of the belief that organs died separately among the
elderly, but Durand-Fardel more typically tried to join the growing
accuracy in pathology with related accuracy in diagnosis. Brain
tumors thus caused a higher percentage of convulsions than brain
softening. Statistics were also offered on the number of apoplexy
victims whose face was pale as opposed to convulsed, and in general
study of face and eyes was urged as a predictor of brain problems.
Durand-Fardel fought a common notion that a strong pulse in a stroke
victim denoted greater likelihood of a second attack, offering figures
that showed no relation between pulse and renewed attack; he
similarly opposed the idea that thin people were more prone to
brain hemorrhage, citing 69 cases in which the victims were most
commonly heavy and apparently healthy before they were felled.
Doctors were told how to use the stethoscope to distinguish between
catarrh and emphysema. They were warned that simple-minded notions,
such as the idea that pneumonia always caused delirium among older
people, had to be discarded in favor of subtler diagnosis.[20]

Finally the new attention to older people as a special medical
category and the interest in fairly predictable organic deterioration
led to a host of caveats against common therapeutic practices, on the
general theme that what will work for an adult may not for an
older person, whose system was weakened, and that some treatments
were positively harmful. Almost everyone urged the mildest
possible remedies, and a realization that the old cure more slowly
than adults. Durand-Fardel noted the temptation to react with panic
to a stroke or brain hemorrhage, causing doctors to bleed the victim;
in fact bleeding was normally counterindicated, for it could not
affect the hemorrhage and only weakened the patient, heightening
the chance of pneumonia . Sometimes one had to admit there was
nothing to do but let nature take its course. Senile gangrene was an
example: here it was best not to operate, for the risk of mortality
was greater than with the disease itself, but rather to 'abandon to

nature the job of separating the decayed from the living parts.' (In fact
the only surgery discussed for older people remained dilation of the
bladder and depression of the prostate.)[21] Many urged attention to
secondary effects, which followed from attention to deterioration of the
system though not of course from the belief in organic discreteness.
Durand-Fardel wanted regular attention to urine and chest for any old
person confined to bed, because of the possibility of retention of toxins
and pneumonia. If urine was insufficient the catheter should be used;
if the chest congested, warm drinks and steam to stimulate spit.
The most common advice was directed against massive bleedings, of the
kind still accepted for adults, not only when the patient had suffered
a stroke but also when auscultation indicated a weak heart. Second on
the danger list were strong emetics, which might enfeeble an elderly
patient further or, at the least, given the general deterioration of the
system, have no effect.[22] Charcot warned against the charlatans who
used colchicum for gout, for this caused stomach problems and
slowed the pulse. Baths, the remedy of the Ancients, were attacked for
they risked apoplexy if hot, heart problems if cold. The challenge to
common practices was without question the most concrete
contribution of geriatric research to the potential health of older
people throughout the nineteenth century.[23]

But here we return to the real medical dilemma, the gap between
innovative research and therapeutics. Pinel, in 1802, urged just as
strongly against massive bleedings and emetics as did Durand-Fardel
fifty years later. This suggests the tragic persistence of these
treatments in common practice, but also the fact that the new
research had not been particularly necessary to produce any
therapeutic improvements. Only in promptings toward concern for
secondary symptoms was the mid-century researcher different from his
predecessors, and this followed more from attention to the actual
incidence of diseases like pneumonia in hospital settings than from the
detailed analysis of organic lesions. Therapeutics changed almost not at
all, and in fact many writers failed to follow through on their own
good advice against unduly drastic traditional measures. For doctors
simply could not sit back and let nature take its course; they believed
that they could help; and yet the new research pointed to no new
treatments, at most reinforcing the traditional stress on preventive
hygiene that might slow organic deterioration. In principle two
general approaches were discussed as particularly appropriate for older
people, again without much change from 1800 to 1870. Stimulants
were needed for systems that lacked the resistance of an adult — hence

light wine, quinquina, caffeine, digitalis were suggested from strokes through pneumonia.[24] Second, purgatives were required to rid the system of toxins, though some urged mildness here too, against irritants such as aloe pills.[25] Laxatives, massages to encourage sweat again cropped up as treatments for virtually every disorder. Durand-Fardel wanted stroke victims to be induced to defecate when first unconscious, for getting rid of foreign matter would clear the ciruclation even in the head. Two points about this approach. First, it was highly unspecific. None of Durand-Fardel's precision in diagnosing types of brain disease shows up in his positive therapeutic recommendations. Second, it followed not from the organic work being stressed in research but from more traditional, though by no means entirely inaccurate, beliefs in the accumulation of toxins or, as even Durand-Fardel noted, veinous blood.

The therapeutics thus related to the continued belief in the dangers of menopause, which prevented proper elimination of waste, or to the idea that ulcers and hemorrhoids might best be left untreated in older people because they too encouraged elimination whose cessation might cause congestion in the lungs or brain. And this in turn was linked to the fact that few of the researchers who discussed treatment at all — and we must remember that many simply dissected after death — could resist the temptation to bleed. Durand-Fardel remained true to his insistence that no general bleeding be undertaken with the elderly, but he wanted local bleeding, close to the problem area, in almost every case. With brain hemorrhage apply leeches to the neck, along with the inevitable purgatives and sinapisms. For apoplexy, so long as the heart was sound, a series of small bleedings. The common use of cauteries and vesicatories was mildly deplored, as likely to weaken the patient, but again neither Durand-Fardel nor Reveillé-Parise could definitely prohibit the practice in serious cases — one had to try something, and getting rid of toxic congestion seemed the only approach. Bleeding was also suggested as the best preventive where there were symptoms of a possible stroke. Bronchitis? Bouillon and syrups to encourage spit, but again bleed the patient too. Catarrh? A bitter drink to prevent its affecting heart or lung, the inevitable laxative, and if fever set in, a bleeding. Pneumonia? Bouillon, wine, Sedlitz water plus bleeding, emetics and vesicatories on the thigh. All of this was very little different from Millot at the century's beginning; he too cautioned against frequent bleeding and emetics and was actually more consistent in opposing bleeding as a killer of old people; but even he could not resist vomitives, along with laxatives, to get rid of bad humors in cases of apoplexy.[26]

The gap between research and therapy had some further consequences, for the researchers were by no means stupid and they suffered from the deaths they witnessed. Reveillé-Parise, urging that disease be fought as soon as it was spotted, because of the lack of resistance of the elderly, had to note that this same low recuperation left the doctor 'few resources in the late season of life.' He toyed with the idea of new treatment, if further study were devoted to the elderly specifically; could not a gas revivify the lungs (whose deterioration he held to be the first cause of aging) just as gases could paralyze them? But for now, nothing; he even attacked the use of cosmetics as making the elderly look ridiculous, barely approving the employment of false teeth or eyes so long as these were not part of a futile effort to appear young. Even Durand-Fardel, more comprehensive in his attempt to suggest remedies, offered no innovations and admitted with real sorrow that many diseases were beyond the physician's power in the case of the elderly; so all one could do was keep statistics on when and how people died.[27]

The nature of the French approach and its weaknesses can be illustrated by specific reference to the heart, for here, even aside from therapy, the focus on organic atrophy itself was misleading.[28] Millot noted early in the century that many older patients complained of pains in their left arm, but he dropped the matter after this reference. Rauzier, a full century later, noted that heart attacks were possible though quite rare.[29] In between, Durand-Fardel stated that heart problems were uncommon among the elderly (noting also that where they existed there was nothing that could be done), while a few pages later reporting that of 149 people dead of various causes 55 had an ossified aorta.[30] Only Josué,[31] early in the twentieth century, was to begin serious study of heart problems among the elderly, as opposed to vascular disorders, but his work was largely derivative of efforts, starting with pathology on normal as well as senile animals, launched in other countries. Why the blindness, when organic analysis had been the key focus of geriatric research in France? The heart was found, in autopsies, more normally enlarged than atrophied; it was assumed this meant it was compensating effectively for vascular impediments. Old age meant atrophy, decay; an organ that normally grew must somehow be exempt from this process and not worth serious pathological analysis. So the heart muscle itself was not, until Josué, subjected to the searching study given to brain, lung and liver. Fortunately in actual clinical practice the general treatises urged attention to the heart as a secondary symptom; Durand-Fardel and, in greater detail, Rauzier both dealt with this, though even here their recommendations were complicated by the belief that the enlarged heart was normal and that auscultation was therefore far less clear for the elderly than for adults. Research, and to a lesser extent clinical practice and certainly the study of possible treatment were severely retarded by the French approach; indeed, cardiac research in France lags to this day.

It would be anachronistic to criticize the overall French approach too severely, at least in its early phases. France was not backward in treatment at mid-century, except in its heavy reliance on bleeding. The point is not to take facile pot shots at doctors, particularly in this area where advance remains limited even now and given the fact that this was a branch of medicine that was not receiving concentrated attention among researchers generally. But we must note the durability of the French approach and the assumptions wrapped up in it, which is why the early period commands attention. Work after 1870 would only confirm the limitations, which by then were becoming unnecessary.

Even at mid-century alternatives were suggested. We can leave aside the Montpellier school, which attacked the Parisian dissecters for forgetting the intangible soul — to the durable detriment of the school's scientific reputation.[32] More interesting was the 1856 work of Dr Turck in Strasbourg.[33] He also blasted the exclusively pathological interests of the Parisians, for he wanted the diseases of old age cured. Turck insisted that the elderly could enjoy Ciceronian wisdom if they were healthy, though he shared the pessimism about the actual conditions of old people in his day. He urged cosmetics for a youthful appearance and wanted to explore a range of new therapies, ranging from restorative hibernation to electrical treatment, which he insisted could revive 'nervous fluids' and thus restore hair color, and tone up skin and body. Turck finally wanted experiments on animals to determine the effectiveness of medicine. Other therapeutic approaches were suggested. In 1857 Edouard Robin recommended lactic acid to break up mineral matter in the body, but this was not taken up again until after 1900.

Equally firmly were the implications of biological advances ignored, from the eighteenth-century interest in plant regeneration through the discoveries of Claude Bernard in the field of internal secretion, and well beyond.[34] This contrasted with developments in other medical

fields, such as obstetrics where biological findings were taken up
quickly at the research level; the bias against old age could not be
overridden. Yet Flourens, in the Buffon tradition, insisted human
longevity could be improved as early as mid-century;[35] his own work
on bone grafts in animals pointed the way toward possible new
therapy. But mainstream French medicine resolutely ignored these
scattered suggestions that the organic burdens of old age might be
alleviated. Again, what might be excusable around 1850 hardened
into an outlook that would long resist alternative views, no matter
how solid their base, contributing to a medical culture and to a
general view of aging which were ultimately counterproductive.

For nineteenth-century research in France, more than in most
countries, reinforced the preponderant classical view of aging as a
time of unrelieved decay. This involved overgeneralization of the
symptoms of aging as well as a reluctance, however agonized, to turn
to research on possible new therapies as opposed to the more
immediately scientific and psychologically less taxing investigation
of lesions in autopsies.

The sources of this approach were numerous. First and foremost,
again, was the classical medical view itself, which held that nature
set clear limits to life and could not be violated. Obviously this
process could not really be disturbed. Boy-Tessier in the 1890s warned
against 'meddlesome interference' with senile brain problems, for
'it is rare that the old man can make active use of his brain.'[36] It was
indeed difficult to shake off the idea that old age was itself a disease.
In a specific case, Durand-Fardel judged emphysema the result of
prolonged use of the lung, which is why it was almost natural. Tradition
showed most clearly in the association of aging with cessation of
sexual activities, for Galen had launched a pervasive belief in
arguing that loss of sexual fluid was loss of the vital fluid.[37] In 1919
Dr Armengaud believed he proved decisively that men who tried
to engage in sexual activity after sixty risked their lives, for in a small
sample of wealthy businessmen he found a higher incidence of death
among those who ignored his advice to abstain than in those who
did, and again the reason was the close association of life and
with the vital fluid, a view expressed just as coherently by Millot
over a century before.[38] Traditionalism thus prompted a vast amount
of bad advice concerning sexual abstinence and in the case of
women was unrelieved by any attention to actual sexual desires
during and after menopause (save for the mention of possible but
dangerous eroticism during menopause itself).[39] Small wonder that

research was directed toward the decay process, including atrophy of the genital organs, rather than to therapeutics, or that such research largely confirmed the classic view.

The classical heritage and the new research approach thus neatly combined in France, not uniquely but with particular vehemence. The dominance of Paris, with its large hospitals for the poor, helps explain the peculiar stress. Suspicion of tampering with nature had been heightened by unsuccessful experiments with Harvey's blood transfusions in the eighteenth century, which had resulted in a government ban on such efforts. Moreover autopsies were legally prohibited until 24 hours after death, which encouraged the belief in organic degeneration, as bodies were often badly preserved. In sum a combination of institutional factors made French geriatrics unusually abstract.[40]

And so the more fruitful alternative of biological research and animal experiments was not taken up by doctors. Josué was the first to use zoology extensively in his work on the senile heart around 1900, but he was belatedly copying British and German examples.[41] Doctors claimed science for their part, as in the statistical approach, but they lacked the sophistication for handling these tools. The early interest in geriatrics here may have been a positive drawback. Durand-Fardel 'proved' that brain hemorrhage was most common between 70 and 79 by citing 26 cases. Diversity of results was commonly ignored in the effort to attain catchy generalizations. Durand-Fardel again reported 22 of 94 individuals over 60, dead of various causes, who had normal blood vessels in their brains but then proceeded to generalize about inevitable vascular decay in the brain. A great temptation to philosophize also pervaded the profession, as in geriatric efforts elsewhere.[42] The French sought a single first cause of aging, the details of which need not concern us; the result was quarrels over whether respiration or the development of conjunctive tissue in complex cells or glandular secretions held pride of place. Rare was the discussion of aging that did not spend as much time on first causes as on possible therapy. Add one final ingredient: a rooted belief that urbanization made natural aging impossible – as Boy-Tessier put it, rural people are 'less oppressed by the exigencies of our epoch' – and one has the mix of hopelessness with which the research level of French medicine confronted the aging process.[43]

Little of this significantly differentiates France from other countries until the late nineteenth century; indeed, as we have contended, France was a leader in geriatric pathology. But after 1880 this research lead, which, we must stress again, had little bearing on living humans, waned because of its own sterility. A doctor in 1886[44] argued against a set age for senility; this was an individual matter. But he could not carry his approach through, for soon he was talking about motor problems everyone had by 60 or the fact that 'the' 70-year old could exert only 35 percent of the hand muscle pressure of the adult. The search for generalization continued. Léri in 1906,[45] picking up from an excellent short article that urged distinction between senility and normal old age,[46] began his long study of the senile brain by noting that such a brain resulted from distinct lesions; the normal brain atrophied but did not suffer from lesions. But by the end of the book the senile brain was clearly the characteristic brain of anyone over 60, due to 'arterial irritation.'[47]

With this ongoing culture, it was almost inevitable that geriatric research diminished in innovative quality as it picked up immensely in quantity between 1870 and 1914. A rapidly expanding medical profession was the basic cause of the new quantity; one dissertation after another measured the deterioration of one organ or function after another. Léri unwittingly demonstrated the growing poverty of pathological research. Able now to perform four to five autopsies a week at the Bicêtre he demolished one by one the generalizations about the state of the senile brain that had been built up since before Durand-Fardel. Dilation of the brain vessels for example was far less common than thought, and it was partially caused by death itself and therefore exaggerated by observations in autopsy. Paralyzed and non-paralyzed people could have the very same brain lesions. There was one note of promise; study of prior symptoms, including examination of the retina, might allow prediction of brain damage; we can 'foresee and perhaps even prevent subsequent difficulties.'[48] But this was not followed up, as Léri went from one exception to any pathological generalization to another only to emerge with a restatement of the conventional view of old people: by 75 the mental state is always modified, with behavior ranging from frequent weeping to possible delirium.

Of course there was new knowledge in the vast outpouring of work. It was recognized that the old could in fact suffer from tuberculosis; the symptoms were simply more gradual.[49] Diagnosis had advanced, as in the use of electrocardiograms. The range of treatments advised against had increased, and this remained important. Both Rauzier and Pic and Bonnamour in the early 1900s condemned the use of vesicatories in pneumonia cases, recommending sinapisms instead, and

optimism about curing pneumonia had grown. Even purgatives were
now seen as too harsh, with laxative washes preferred, and the recourse
to laxatives was itself less common at the onset of disease.[50] Use of
digitalis for heart problems was up by the turn of the century; the old
were now more commonly found operable for cancer (now seen as a
major disease among the elderly), and Rauzier could give success
rates for each type of operation performed on patients over 60.[51] But
still there was a strong dose of traditionalism; Rauzier recommended
bleeding for severe apoplexy (or the use of leeches if the patient was very
old). And the limitations of treatment were constantly stressed.
Boy-Tessier, after saying that normal senility could be delayed more
than was commonly realized, noted that old people often refused
to change their life patterns and dropped the subject of therapy. Rauzier
saw no hope for the paralyzed victim of a stroke; he could not be
retrained, for an old person was 'scarcely apt for acquisitions and
transformations.' Senile madness similarly had to be left untouched,
for the old refused guidance.[52]

The most promising French development was in fact scorned by the
French. Following from the traditional association of sexual activity
and aging, Brown-Séquard in the late 1870s began experiments on
himself with solutions derived from ground-up animal testicles. In his
publications a decade later he noted: 'I have regained at least all the
strength which I possessed some years back.'[53] But he encountered
little but ridicule from his coprofessionals who held that there was no
reversing the now-fabled deterioration of the organs.[54] Hence Rauzier,
in his treatise, dismissed hormone injections as 'having failed to keep
their marvelous promise'[55] — and this by the time that they were
being widely and successfully used in the United States, Germany and
elsewhere. Metchnikoff's elaborate search for a lactic chemical to
attack the *macrophages* in the large intestine, which he found the cause
of human aging, received more deserved scorn, though one biologist
(not a doctor) approved in general of 'the idea of coming to the aid
of an organism struggling against usury.'[56] A physician expressed a
more common view in 1903, with a distinctive justification: medicine
cannot control aging, and it should not even if it could; for it was
good for society to love and respect old, useless people, so if senility
were prevented the commonwealth would suffer.[57] French geriatric
research inevitably lagged farther and farther behind as emphasis
elsewhere switched to the heart, to diagnosis, and to possible
treatments.[58]

It is vital for the social history of medicine to recognize the possible gap between the publishing researcher and the ordinary practitioner, between level one and level two in our initial outline. The admonitions of the researchers suggest that the gap in this case often operated against the best interests of the health of older people, however well-intentioned the practitioner. Bleeding and the use of depressants must have been all too common; some indeed recommended bleeding even of healthy subjects as a precaution, to get rid of toxins. In one area, however, general practitioners,[59] in contact with a wide range of patients and not just those in extreme debility, took a more benign view of the early stages of aging than the researchers did. Menopause was not viewed with great alarm by most of the ordinary doctors who wrote for a non-professional audience. Gujétant in 1836 urged that women realize menopause is a natural process for which harsh remedies should be avoided; death rates did not rise. Women should combine resignation with frequent visits to a doctor, who would perform small bleedings against the possibility of hemorrhage, adding treatment by vesicatory if the subject was nervous.[60] In an updated version of this tradition Vinoy, at about the same time Rauzier dismissed hormones, was recommending hormonal treatment for menopausal women, along with psychological counseling for self-mastery, in the rare cases when menopause caused serious problems.[61]

But if ordinary practitioners struck a happier note on the preliminaries of old age, they were at least as likely as the researchers to throw up their hands when confronted with the problems of old age itself. Hence they so often overreacted with bleeding or use of strong vapors when dealing with serious disease. The common use of harsh purgatives resulted from a similar belief that the inertia of old organs required particularly strong stimuli; many strokes resulted but the practice continued because of the hopelessness with which doctors confronted old age.[62] Pétron described how gout could attack the heart, killing in just a few hours. Cancer was a blood poison that might be attacked with vesicatories, but normally only palliation of pain, through opiates, was possible. Wine was widely recommended, 'the milk of old men,' save by a few who warned it might stir up passions. But all this is to say that the ordinary doctor probably combined a bit of superstition with a bit of mild treatment, sometimes overreacting to emergencies, but offering no special wisdom on the health problems of the old. At best, as with Pétron, there was a sense that ordinary treatment might be too harsh for the old. But there was also a firm conviction, based really on the same culture that the researchers elaborated more fully, that old age tied the doctor's hands. Hence Pétron viewed 75 as the onset of extreme old age, essentially a gradual death which the physician could not prevent, 'for it is not within the doctor's power to prolong life beyond its term.' Unaware of surgery, for example, Pétron saw nothing to do in cases of retention of urine save to keep patients clean, 'to prevent greater sufferings and prolong for a bit their feeble existence.'[63] Add to this a heavy use of opiates, particularly belladonna which was held to be least constipating, and mineral baths for the wealthy, and the medical arsenal was exhausted.[64]

Hence the amazing fact that despite massive unemployment among French doctors, ranging up to 25 percent, no geriatric specialty developed in practice until after 1950. Doctors, often to their great sorrow, had nothing to offer even as other specializations like gynecology and pediatrics began to flourish. And patients knew this, so an obvious channel of professional advancement was itself atrophied.

Toward 1900 there were some signs of reaction against their therapeutic impotence, for ordinary doctors could easily be tempted by their own agonized feelings, as well as a desire for a good reputation, to try something that worked; and the variety of quality and approach was undoubtedly greater than in formal research. One doctor calmly wrote, in 1908, of his regular use of testicular serums and psychotherapy instead of the bleeding and the traditional medicines of the elderly.[65] But by his own account he was unusual. More representative was Dr Ferran, in Lyons, who urged alkaloid derivatives from plants, in small regular doses, to prevent both of what he saw to be the most common causes of death among the elderly, pneumonia and a senile weakening of the nervous system. But Ferran too, for all his zeal, had to note the resistance of his 'classical confrères,' the 'official mandarins,' who insisted on conventional remedies, including the cold baths of the ancients, even when highly inappropriate, and who really believed that a sick old person would die no matter what was done. And Ferran himself noted that bleeding should be administered in cases of brain hemorrhage; and though he cited Charcot in discussing rheumatism he recommended treatments which the master had specifically advised against.[66] Nothing of course can capture the variety of practices used by ordinary doctors in treating the elderly, but with rare exception they followed from the general culture and not uncommonly did more harm than good.

Finally, we come to the subjects of this varied medical interest. As we have noted, most old people did not see doctors before 1914. Most were still rural and many urban elderly moved back to the country,

out of normal medical access, well into the twentieth century. Some
may have shown good sense in realizing that medicine had little to
offer them. But there was a strain of hope as well which might lead
some to doctors but many also to charlatans. Human fat was sold by
itinerant vendors, at considerable cost, to treat rheumatism. The
'vin de Dr Chatel' was advertised for those who felt weak with age;
many must have turned to those who claimed to be able to cure
cancer without surgery.[67] In 1873 a widely sold pamphlet told how
to live to be a hundred: start a child off well by salting him heavily,
washing the salt away after a few days; wear precious stones; drink
milk, for lactic acid delays ossification; sleep with one's head facing
north in tune with magnetic currents — in sum a traditional mixture
of nonsense with some advice doctors would approve.[68]

Charlatanage persisted basically because the cures made about as
much sense as those recommended by medical science. What we are
dealing with involves three factors: (1) dislike of some things
doctors did; (2) a sense of fatalism about dying, so vivid in the
working class, which doctors shared and reinforced; but (3) a
periodic belief in some miracle cure. An ambiguous popular culture,
but one we still maintain.

As to point (1), the disparity between what research physicians
had been interested in and what old people were suffering from showed
up painfully when death statistics finally began again to be issued
in the 1920s. In 1926 (and the figures were only slightly different
a decade later) heart disease annually killed 0.5 percent of the male
population aged 60-70, 1.0 percent over 70. Strokes followed, at
0.3 percent and 0.9 percent. Pneumonia and other respiratory
ailments, 0.3 percent and 0.8 percent; cancer 0.3 percent and
0.5 percent. Senility, 0.4 percent and 1.5 percent. Of these major
killers, geriatric doctors had been investigating only strokes directly.
Senility was a convenient catch-all for lack of more precise
diagnosis. Cancer had been discussed, pneumonia was certainly
well known but essentially without human remedy, heart disease
had been ignored almost entirely. So why go to a doctor? The situation
in 1946, when adult longevity was beginning to improve, saw an
increase in cancer rate (0.5 percent and 0.9 percent for the two
age categories), stability in heart diseases and strokes; but a massive
decline in pneumonia and respiratory disease (0.2 percent and
0.3 percent) and in death from senility (0.3 percent and 0.5 percent).
Here at last was a beginning of a reason to consult doctors,
particularly for chest infections; but geriatric specialists had not

produced this result. Sulfa drugs, followed by antibiotics, had not been pioneered by people primarily interested in the elderly, or, for that matter, by French doctors of any sort. The decline in deaths due to senility, particularly before age 69, followed from some possible refinement in doctors' definition of the cause of death but also from improved general living conditions (even in the rag-tag year 1946); doctors could claim little credit. It was in fact the increased vitality of the elderly that put pressure on doctors, for a non-senile 70-year-old could legitimately expect cures, not placebos or pain-killers. And here we can turn to the more human side of medical care, going back first to the unstatistical nineteenth century itself.

Some people with early access to doctors specifically rebelled against the more painful treatments normally used; Pétron for example reported reluctance, particularly among women, to have vesicatories applied in cancer cases. And this of course was quite sensible. There was similar resistance to catheters among men, though with severe bladder problems this usually yielded to necessity where a knowledgable doctor was available at all. Perhaps most indicative of attitudes among the popular classes was the continued reluctance to enter *hospices,* those hospitals particularly set aside for the elderly. We have firm figures only for the 1850s onward. But from then until the 1920s there was no increase, in fact a *per capita* decrease, in the percentage of the population over 60 who entered *hospices.* In the 1870s even the absolute number declined. And this despite growing urbanization, which held the possibility of diminution in familial support. Paris stands out as the single exception, but only after 1875; and only after 1900 is the increase in the hospitalized elderly in Paris large enough to exclude the probability that it was drawn mainly from the provinces with doctors referring particularly stubborn cases; only after 1900, in other words, that an increasing percentage of Paris' elderly consented to enter hospitals even when seriously ill. The belated shift in attitude was particularly pronounced among women; from being a minority of the *hospice* population in mid-century, despite their preponderance in the elderly population as a whole, women became a strong majority by the 1920s, and again earlier than this in Paris.[69]

In this pattern of behavior the general populace was behaving quite logically, abetted by a traditional dislike of dying in hospitals which was also quite sensible. Following from the actual medical practice and culture which we have described, mortality rates in the *hospices* improved slowly and belatedly, though Paris led the way, perhaps less through superior therapeutics than better diagnostic procedures,

including very simple ones such as Charcot's regular temperature-taking.
Death rates annually were about 19 percent in the 1850s, still over
18 percent in the 1880s, back up over 20 percent in the early 1890s.
By 1921 they were down to 17 percent, and in Paris 11 percent; here
was a minor breakthrough, the first worth recording in the actual
history of this contrast between formal medicine and the elderly in
modern times.

All of which means that in a certain sense there is very little social
history of geriatric medicine until the twentieth century; medicine was
not directly interacting with most older people. Hence the sticky life
expectancy rates among adults — 60 for males 1817-31 at age 20,
69.9 at age 50; 61.2 and 70.2 in the 1860s; 61.0 and 69.8 at the turn
of the century — follow from the limitations of geriatric medicine and
the fact that these inhibited most older people from seeking
professional assistance. New knowledge was not prolonging life as the gap
between major killers and pathological research indicated, all part of a
vicious circle which kept doctors busily finding out what had caused a
death, and caused patients to keep away from doctors, save when dire
poverty forced them into the *hospices* really as a last refuge, preferable
to dying in the street. Those old people who did consult physicians
around the turn of the century clearly shared specific aspects of the
traditional medical approach, combined with a desire for something
dramatic to relieve their ills. They could not wait to use harsh
purgatives, believing constipation the cause of a host of illnesses, much
to the vexation of those doctors who were rethinking the advisability
of this practice for the elderly.[70] Perhaps a similar cultural
correspondence involves the reporting of symptoms of heart trouble.
Many doctors pointed out how rare it was for an old person to
indicate heart problems; at most a few called attention to palpitation
or dyspepsia. In other words, before it became a widely recognized
killer among the elderly it seemed pointless to make too much of pain,
which in turn retarded research on senile heart disease.[71] In this case
and others it is clear that, overall, French geriatrics and the
stagnating health conditions of the elderly were locked in a common
culture around 1900, in which doctors and old people (whether patients
or not) could easily feed each other's pessimism.

If the modern social history of geriatrics begins only after 1920, in terms
of frequent interaction between older people and doctors, this was
initially due to changes in the position and outlook of the elderly rather
than a new geriatric medicine. The impact of patients on medicine, too

often ignored, is vital to recognize here. Shortly before World War One the state extended free hospital care to the elderly poor. This was one important cause of the wider *per capita* use of hospitals from the 1920s onward. Groups of old people drawn from the middle class and some better-paid workers formed at the same time, and evinced a definite interest in improved health. Yet French medicine was slow to respond. The sluggish mortality rates in the provincial *hospices* in the 1920s suggest this. More generally life expectancy for 20-year-olds, particularly males, changed only modestly in the interwar years — the big break was after 1946 — while for 50-year-olds the watershed was later still: only by the 1950s could a man of fifty expect well over twenty years more life.[72] Obviously factors other than medical were involved both in stagnancy and in subsequent improvement, but medicine played a role.

For most French doctors, following a different drum, lost formal interest in the elderly between the wars. France's lagging birth rate encouraged ever greater concentration on child-bearing and pediatrics. Equally important, the growing myopia in research on the elderly led now to a diminution not only of creativity but also to a positive reduction in the amount of research conducted. Decay had been sufficiently charted, and there was little more to do. Few theses emerged, after the previous outpouring, until the 1930s, and even then France's relative lag was not reversed. Shock's extensive bibliography on gerontology, which reaches well back into the 1920s, contains few French references, and almost nothing before 1950. A major Italian geriatric survey in 1938 similarly cites virtually no French work after World War One, with the important exception of biological rather than medical studies.[73] The very fact that there was no French geriatric treatise between 1912 and 1957 indicates something of the level of interest. Even more to the point, French researchers resuming work on geriatrics from the end of the 1930s onward had little but foreign study to fall back on. New attention to the brain, in the early 1950s, brought laments that so little had been done on healing, as opposed to pathology. A monograph on changes in the eye cited but sixteen French works, as opposed to 46 in foreign languages.[74] The first contemporary survey of geriatrics similarly had to rely heavily on foreign research. Whole sections on the effects of age on the senses, on digestion, on cancer, and on arteriosclerosis contain only one or two French references in substantial bibliographies.[75] More work could be cited on bone diseases, including rheumatism and lung problems, but no chapter contains more than a minority of French references. No geriatric journal was founded in France until the 1950s, by which time Italy had four, Germany (where the first was launched, in 1936) at least eight, and so on. Until the 1940s the foreign work that was being done passed France by. A thesis on senile heart problems, deriving from Lyons, the one center in which studies of aging maintained any consistency, had to note that the scattered French research on the heart had remained purely anatomical, tracing the lesions after death, and was thus bypassed by American and other studies of diagnosis (particularly the use of the electrocardiogram) and medication. And the thesis itself, though discussing three forms of diagnosis in detail, remained largely anatomical in focus.[76]

As before, there were individual deviations from the norm. A doctor in the 1920s cited virtually every possible therapy, in addition to conventional and sound advice on hygiene: oxygen in cases of pneumonia, medication against hypertension, extracts from animal glands to tone up any deficient organ, tissue grafts that made it possible to imagine the day when a heart might be transplanted all led Dr Vidal to conclude that 'we are close to solving the problem of rejuvenation, sensibly understood.'[77] But this optimism was lost amid a welter of indifference. Only in one area did research and therapy make consistent advance in France until the last two or three decades. The traditional approach to menopause was cast aside in favor of active treatment. Here the thesis writers were active, proclaiming the possibility of new therapy; their findings were incorporated into every gynecological survey and were welcomed by most general practitioners, who had always taken a less catastrophic view of the phenomenon in any event.[78] To be sure, a woman doctor writing in 1923 — as so often the case, harder on her sex than men — offered little help to the menopausal woman, who was embarked on inevitable physical decline: 'they can do no better than to bow before an ineluctable destiny, aiding themselves by a consoling philosophy to support this change without bitterness.'[79] There was some quarrel over whether hormones were really effective into the late 1920s, but few doctors rejected innovation out of hand. Even ovarian grafts were considered when hormones (still often insufficiently refined) failed to have sufficient or durable effects. Also, of course, there was increased vigilance against uterine cancer, which was routinely operable if caught in time. Where menopause offered no dramatic symptoms, the traditional approach long continued to dictate neglect of hormonal treatment.[80] But by the 1950s estrogen was recommended even for minor problems, with the women assured that, her hormonal balance restored, she would pass into a harmonious and active phase of life.[81]

Old age itself, however, was given no such fillip. The doldrums into which geriatric research had fallen were amply confirmed in general medical practice. A medical manual of 1937, urging hormonal therapy for problems in menopause, returned to recommendations of bleeding in cases of apoplexy, with the reduced tolerance of the elderly recognized only in the advice that purely local treatment be administered, through leeches.[82] Another compendium recommended cold baths for heart patients who were obese, thus proving that, no matter how many patients fell by the wayside, every classical precept was carefully kept alive.[83] As in politics, the French seemed to forget no past approach. Similarly, purgatives were held at the ready for any illness. More generally many doctors urged the evil effects of city life on longevity, recommending early retirement to the countryside, and some could not help repeating the old advice that post-menopausal women abstain from sexual activity.[84] Of course there were changes. French doctors widely adopted sulfa drugs by the late 1930s, which resulted in the dramatic reduction in deaths among the elderly from pneumonia.[85] But these innovations were part of a patchwork, not a rethinking of the approach to aging. Hence as late as 1948 a manual might diligently recommend sulfa drugs and vitamins while condemning hormones as ineffective, except in menopause, urging bleeding against hypertension and other disorders, repeating Charcot's idea that organs age separately, warmly commending magnesium salts against cancer, and urging sexual abstinence as old age was a 'time to purify one's thoughts and live chastely in the esteem of one's family and friends.'[86]

In this essentially conservative medical atmosphere there was ample room for continued charlatanage and oversimplification, for if most doctors would not innovate others, both in and out of the profession, were ready. Change was in the air, if not in most consulting rooms. The number of old people rose steadily as the simple effect of previous population growth. Limited improvements in living conditions and pension arrangements allowed some, at least, to contemplate the desirability of better medical care. The pages of retirees' magazines — themselves the sign of new consciousness — were dotted with advertisements for wonder drugs. *Le Cri du retraité* soberly reproduced articles by doctors listing the symptoms of senile decay and offering no remedies save conventional hygiene; but they also embraced columns on the marvelous properties of magnesium salts to cure problems of the skin, anxiety, prostitis, and cancer, while advertisements heralded 'phosphoneurium' to reconstitute one's nervous system and Radiomuth pills to prevent brain hemorrhage. *Guérir,* a popularized science magazine, was even more explicit in its belief that old age could be fought: 'Everyone knows that old age is only a word when all functions well in the human machine.' The way to push back senility? — magnesium salts, so warmly commended by Dr Delbet for their ability to reconstitute cells, give new *élan* to the kidneys, and of course prevent cancer and prostate problems.[87] Another doctor legitimized a second popular approach during the period, the alignment with nature that would allow one to live past a hundred in beauty and health. Classical medicine worked on anatomies, on dead bodies, not on life. The earth was the vital source, and by aligning with it — and particularly by rubbing oneself gently along the lines of the earth's motion — one could live long and vigorously. The doctor, in perfect health at age 75, modestly likened his discovery to that of Copernicus.[88] An outright charlatan advertised that he could prolong life for anyone who sent him some recently cut hair; in a trance, his personal magnetism would withdraw all ailments. Less noxiously, 'Professor' Mono, in Toulouse, widely publicized a vegetarian diet; illness did not exist, just auto-intoxication, which could be cured by natural elements, notably vitamins and phosphorous, that would rebuild the cells. The Professor violated conventional medicine still further by claiming that a person should remain vital until 80, able among other things to procreate. But the medical profession was alert; Mono was charged with fraud and imprisoned.[89] Efforts to capitalize on the desire for new therapies for the diseases of old age easily confirmed the mainstream doctors in their self-righteous traditionalism.

For change could not come from within formal French medicine, and a dosage of borderline charlatanism proved to be one of the sources of innovation. French geriatrics needed a re-ordering before it could provide much service to the elderly. It needed to believe in treatment as well as having better treatments to offer; the two were intertwined. The sterility of geriatric research by the 1920s confirmed the need for change, but it did not provide a source for it.

Advances in research and therapy made in other countries formed an ongoing framework for change. It was difficult to ignore such work entirely, and as we have seen, it provided a basis for French geriatrics by the later 1930s. German and British research was important, but attention was increasingly drawn to Russian gerontologists, such as

Bogolometz, and to American work, for these provided a ringing
optimism about the possibilities of prolonging a vigorous life as well
as a host of specific findings. After World War Two a number of French
medical journals provided regular columns on advances made in
American geriatrics.[90] The imitative factor could be more specific: the
first French eye bank was formed as a direct result of the New York
bank established in 1945, though it long remained more limited in its
activities.[91] America also provided models in plastic surgery. French
plastic surgeons had begun to operate shortly before World War One,
and of course the art got a considerable lift from the needs of the
war itself. But its application to the elderly came only in the 1930s,
and this depended heavily on work across the Atlantic.[92]

An earlier and more direct impulse to a new geriatric approach came
from endocrinology, in which French biologists played a leading role.
In the tradition of Claude Bernard and Brown-Séquard, Gley and
Léopold Lévi continued research on glandular secretions.[93] But,
although some of the experimentation involved humans — Gley, for
example, treated prematurely senile menopausal women — it
remained to link biology with medicine in any general fashion, after
the reception given to Brown-Séquard's efforts a few decades before.
Here, two figures loom large in the interwar period. Alexis Carrel's
discoveries concerning the preservation of tissues had immense
implications for the treatment of disease and organic atrophy in the
elderly. As Carrel himself noted, 'old age without illness will not be
fearsome; it's disease, not old age, that causes most of our
unhappiness.'[94] Ironically Carrel shared several of the beliefs common
to French medical culture. Although a meticulous researcher he had a
great impulse to philosophize (as in his speculations concerning
physiological time, which he likened, not to Copernicus, but to
Einstein). He also believed that modern civilization was severely
detrimental to health and longevity, which is why new action was
needed essentially to bring man into renewed harmony with nature.
But Carrel hated French medical tradition for its narrowness and its
tendency to describe rather than to seek causes and cures, and his
intent was to 'make organisms that don't need repairs; that require
neither doctors nor surgeons.'[95] His outlook stemmed from his
reception in France, which was at best indifferent. His only French
research base was the Institut Pasteur, a private organization which
could only slowly influence public training and research; most of his
work was in fact conducted in the United States, funded by the
Rockefeller Foundation. The same largely held true of his immediate

disciple, Lecomte de Nouy, who also held back from medical
applications directly although writing a book on physics for the use
of doctors.[96]

Following Carrel's lead, Serge Voronoff worked and published
extensively on grafting animal glands to humans for purposes of
rejuvenation; here medicine and biology were finally joined. But
Voronoff was no orthodox French doctor who saw a new light. Born
in Russia and naturalized only in the 1890s, he claimed his initial
inspiration from observing eunuchs in Egypt while he served as court
physician; he was convinced that they aged prematurely and died
young, and of course the secret was glandular. He followed this up by
veterinary work in North Africa, where his glandular grafts were
frequently successful on sheep and cattle; in World War One he
broadened his experience through bone grafts on wounded soldiers.[97]
His work on glandular grafts, which were intended to provide more
durable treatment than the hormones then available, began after 1919,
when he first presented his findings on animals to the Academy of
Medicine.[98] Voronoff's work quickly found imitators. Dartigues began
grafts of the thyroid as well as sex glands, in 1924, and was also
active in plastic surgery. In a related effort Jaworski claimed success
by injecting blood from young people, presumably full of hormones,
into old people suffering from fatigue.[99]

The medical reception given this work was long suspicious. Voronoff
had been overenthusiastic in his 1919 report — 'I have found the
remedy against old age' — and was suitably rebuked. The French
Academy forbade him to speak again in 1922, at which point he
resigned from the French surgical association. His research base was not
a medical school but the experimental chemistry department of the
Collège de France. Many doctors looked askance even at more modest
applications of the findings of endocrinologists: 'the role of hormonal
therapy is fine but it is extremely limited.'[100] Voronoff's findings
began to be used in the Ecole de Médecine only in the early 1930s; in
1932 the doughty Academy awarded a prize to Dartigues for his work
on grafts. But opposition long lingered.[101] A physician advocating
embryo treatments, through hormones and vitamins, to re-establish
the organs and enable man to live out his natural span of one hundred
years, reported widespread opposition from his colleagues in 1950.[102]
Manuals by orthodox physicians in the 1950s admitted the possibility
of hormonal treatment but preserved great skepticism; it was 'too soon'
to decide definitely, and in the meantime conventional hygiene plus
a bit of medication (including now vitamins and preventive doses of

digitalis) constituted the only safe approach.[103] The old should
resign themselves to highly restricted activity, for even gardening was too
risky — stamp collecting and genealogical research were most
appropriate. Another doctor, though praising suitable exercise, including
sexual activity, condemned the optimism of American and Russian
gerontologists, citing with glee the fact that Bogolometz had died at 64:
'After all, these stories of serums maybe are not as serious as people say.'[104]

Gradually, however, advances came. Revived geriatric research from
the late 1930s carefully stressed the need to distinguish between normal
conditions and abnormal lesions, and this time the maxim was adhered to.
Hence the normal senile eye is free from lesions; the sick lung, still a
major killer despite antibiotics, requires serious attention but it is not
the usual condition among the elderly.[105] Belief in therapy became
widespread, and the focus of serious experimentation. Binet worked on
oxygenation and followed the Russian lead in investigating the results
of injections of chicken embryos in improving muscle tone.[106]
Geriatric surgery advanced apace, and the age of normally successful
operability moved back steadily.[107] Doctors played a major role in
promoting the more optimistic attitude about old age generally, after
World War Two, as their American counterparts had done in the
1920s. The old could be creative, active, even (within reason) sexy.
They could expect steady medical advance: 'Every day brings us new
knowledge in this domain.' Already, ill-health had become
unnecessary: 'Aide-toi, tes glandes t'aideront.'[108] Binet in 1956 said
that old age should be 'got in hand' as, he claimed with some justice,
obstetrics had been fifty years before. Destrem, two years later, called
for recognition that long life was normal and could easily be made
pleasant. As we have seen, old age itself was redefined, a particularly
dramatic change in the case of women as menopause and aging were
at last dissociated; 75 or 80 now heralded the onset of active old age,
with senility relegated to the 90s.[109]

The change in approach had become irresistible to most doctors
working and writing on problems of aging. The success of the pioneering
work in France between the wars and the more abundant study abroad
played a major role in the shift. Doctors do want to cure and they are
not insensitive to new specializations that might improve their own
fortunes as well as those of their patients. Within the new research
context the actual incidence of disease among the aged received
attention. It is no accident that after 1940 the French focused more
research on geriatric lung problems and on rheumatism than on
organic lesions or on cancer, for the French had particular difficulties in

these areas; but the contrast with the nineteenth century, where
medical interest had largely followed pathology rather than disease
incidence, is marked.[110] And the growing number of old people
could not be ignored. This could have impinged on doctors'
consciousness even had the percentage seeking medical attention not
changed. In fact the increased percentage entering the *hospices* in the
1920s suggests that the number rose. Léon Binet, who wisely
studied demography as well as medicine, noted this as a major factor
in the new age of French geriatrics.

Finally, perhaps primarily, the elderly themselves played a role in
converting doctors, for news of new cures and new approaches
received early and favorable attention in the press. Newspapers cited
endocrinological work, in 1920, as offering the 'elixir of long life.'[111]
More sedately, retirees' magazines added accounts of hormonotherapy
and plastic surgery to the praise of magnesium salts, by 1936.[112] For,
however surprising to French doctors, the idea of wonder cures
appealed to the traditional, if often repressed, optimistic element
in the popular culture of aging, the Ponce de Leon syndrome.
Indeed during the very years that Carrel and Voronoff were doing their
work, a peasant in Poitou, François Victor, practiced applied
endocrinology as he advised his clients to eat chicken embryos for
rejuvenation. Again the link between traditional popular interest in
cure-alls and modern geriatrics is considerable, above all in that
both had to bypass conventional medical pessimism. The elaborate
accounts of foreign work — American, Swedish, Russian — drew still
more attention after World War Two.[113] Many a doctor reported that
his elderly patients, well-read on medical advances, came in demanding
tissue transplants or serum injections;[114] however distasteful this advice
from below might be, it could not be entirely ignored. In return,
retirees' periodicals for the first time began advocating regular medical
visits as essential to a happy old age.[115]

In the contemporary period, then, a social history of geriatrics
has finally become a reality. Individual researchers helped elaborate
a popular current of expectation for improvement. This promoted
a more general conversion to new approaches. Both, in turn, finally
reacted favorably on the health of the elderly themselves, as the steady
advance in the longevity of mature adults since 1950 abundantly
testifies.

The history of French geriatrics thus had to be one of discontinuity;
the break came unfortunately late for a country whose overall population

was the first to age. It can of course rightly be claimed that conservatism avoided many therapeutic pitfalls and that the ultimate potential of geriatric therapeutics is still clouded by the ineluctable fact of deterioration and death. However judged, the history of French geriatrics remains instructive in several respects. It raises obvious comparative questions, in terms of why and to what degree other countries were free to follow different patterns of development. It contributes to the thorny question of the interaction between doctors and society. Medical culture contributed to or at least paralleled a major stream of popular culture that associated old age with inevitable debility. But doctors were not adapting their outlook to public need or to that strand of popular culture that sought a magical release from suffering. Hence the specific interaction between doctors and the aged long remained limited; doctors in this case were too caught up in a negative culture even to follow through on the dynamic of professionalization and develop a specialization for an obviously definable health group, though of course the limited means of the elderly contributed to this lag.

Indeed geriatrics is still ill-developed in France. French research, though more open than before, is still far from the forefront of innovation. The most comprehensive post-war geriatric survey, though admirable in many respects, continues to stress the anatomical investigation of decay; therapies are noted but receive relatively little space.[116] There is no survey on the care of the aged, as opposed to article-length monographs on specific diseases and their treatment; yet such surveys are numerous in English and German.[117] France lags also in research on the design of geriatric hospitals, on nursing and on rehabilitation. We must ask, then, how fully traditional attitudes have been modified, in medical practice as well as research. We must ask also the extent to which a continuing culture has helped poison the view many elderly take of themselves, creating that expectation of debility and illness which has little necessary relation to reality.[118] If it remains a fledgling field in terms of wide social applicability, geriatrics has a history with which its practitioners should come to terms, not necessarily to reject all elements of past culture but at least to be sure they are conscious of what they retain.

The average French person still lives less long, once attaining adulthood, than people in most industrial countries; life expectancy does exceed that in the United States, but from birth, because of dramatically lower child mortality rates, more than from age 20 or age 50. The comparative differences remain fascinating. At level one, the research tier, Britain and Germany but particularly Russia and the United States have consistently proved more open to innovation in therapy — in Russia's case, both before and after the Revolution. It would be tempting to correlate interest in longevity with general social vitality. So the specific French culture with which we have dealt continues to have human impact and deserve serious re-examination. Yet we are constantly reminded of the common limitations on views of the health of the elderly, where France may serve better as an example than an exception. Many curable diseases go untreated simply because a person is old; people working on dramatic improvements in geriatric medicine still often fringe on quackery.[119]

And one must not be too hard on doctors. Their anguish at being unable to do more for old people was and remains real. Even traditional advice was better than nothing, though the potential elderly, convinced of an early demise, might not listen — as the centenarian said when asked about his lot, 'If I'd known I was going to live this long I would have taken better care of myself.'

Yet the most dramatic conclusion from the recent history of geriatrics in France, if perhaps to a slightly greater extent than in other industrialized countries, is twofold. First, a major improvement in adult longevity in the last thirty years, that is in life expectancy after, say, age fifty. An amazing number of people are unaware of this. We have cited the poll of French people in the post-war period, where the majority believed that people at any age lived less long than in the past; even knowledgable doctors today are unaware of the improvement of approximately a full decade in adult longevity. But the fact is, if you make it to fifty the chances are you'll make it to near-eighty, and this means more old people and an extension of the period of old age.

Second, a great deal of the improvement, within the context of general scientific (not just medical) research, came from new initiatives from elements of the elderly, who picked up the general tendency to fight traditional resignation to pain and disease and pressed their doctors to conform. An incomplete trend, varied by class and limited by what seem to be ineluctable limits on lifespan and average health. But this is our first optimistic note from old people themselves. They proved capable of initiative in a vital area and their desire for a new health base continues. This corresponds to other changes in life-style as the elderly react, if still tentatively, to the conditions of modern society.

Notes

1. Relatedly, the historical literature on medicine dealing with the elderly is, to say the least, extremely sparse. In part this follows from the fact that many of the developments most affecting the elderly occurred within the framework of more general medicine. Many French doctors, for example, improved the analysis of pneumonia or heart problems without establishing a specific geriatric focus. In part, however, the neglect stems from the pattern of specialization within the medical profession itself, in which the elderly, most needing care after infants but most difficult to care for successfully, received no pride of place. Surgical advances inevitably focused first on adults; age-specific medicine as a distinct branch dealt largely with pre-menopausal women. Hence the most elaborate history of French medicine, written in the 1930s, has no section dealing with geriatrics at all, despite the fact that this was an area in which France could long have claimed a lead. Laignet-Lavastine (ed.), *Histoire générale de la médecine,* III (Paris, 1949).
2. Philippe Pinel, *La Médicine clinique* (Paris, 1802); R. Prus, 'Recherches sur les maladies de la vieillesse,' *Mémoires de l'Acamémie royale de médecine* (1840), pp.1-26; Léon Rostan, *Cours de médecin clinique* (Paris, 1930), I, p.79; II, pp.277ff; III, pp.329-31. For an overview though not focusing on geriatrics, see E.H. Ackerknecht, *Medicine at the Paris Hospitals, 1798-1848* (Baltimore, 1967).
3. *Statistique de la France, Mouvement de la Population,* 1900, *passim.*
4. To claim avoidable hypochondria may seem presumptuous, but as we have seen there are strong indications that sense of well-being by retirement age has little necessary relation to health; hence it changes little in a given individual from 60 to 80. See Caisse nationale de retraite des ouvriers du bâtiment et des travaux publics, *Réalités du troisième âge* (Paris, 1968).
5. Prus, 'Recherches,' p.25.
6. *Statistique de la France, Mouvement de la Population,* 1861-1899.
7. See for example the pioneering study by Durand-Fardel, *Traité clinique et pratique des maladies des vieillards* (Paris, 1854).
8. M. Nouche, *Des Maladies de la Vessie* (Paris, 1810).
9. A.J. Landré-Beauvais, *Doit-on admettre une nouvelle espèce de goutte?* (Paris, 1800).
10. See, for example, A. Lacassagne, *La Verte vieillesse* (Lyons, 1920).
11. J.A. Millot, *La Gérocomie* (Paris, 1807).
12. Prus, 'Recherches,' pp.25-6.
13. Charcot, *Leçons cliniques sur les maladies des vieillards* (Paris, 1866).
14. Durand-Fardel, *Traité,* pp.381-2.
15. L.A. Goubelly, *Connoissances necessaires sur la grossesse, sur les maladies laiteuses, et sur la cessation des règles* (Paris, 1785), II, pp.362ff.
16. Xavier Bichat, *Recherches physiologiques sur la vie et la mort* (Paris, 1805), p.143.
17. Pinel, *Médecine, passim.*
18. Millot, *Gérocomie,* pp.351-60.
19. Charcot, *Leçons,* Rostan, *Cours,* II. See also Andre Léri, *le Cerveau sénile* (Lille, 1906), *passim,* which sums up much previous work.
20. Durand-Fardel, *Traité, passim.*
21. *Idem,* p.718.
22. Prus, 'Recherches,' p.6.
23. Charcot, *Leçons,* pp.120ff; Reveillé-Parise, *Traité, passim.*
24. Pinel, *Médecine,* pp.85, 367; M. Beau, 'Etudes cliniques sur les maladies des vieillards,' *Journal de Médecine* (1843), pp.330-7.
25. J.N. Reveillé-Parise, *Traité,* p.186.

26. Durand-Fardel, *Traité*; Millot, *Gérocomie.*
27. Reveillé-Parise, *Traité,* p.263.
28. Lest it seem anachronistic to raise this issue it should be noted that 'hypertrophy' of the heart accounted for almost 10 percent of all female deaths over 60 in 1859, and for 7 percent of male deaths. Though 1860 rates were lower, and pneumonia, tuberculosis, apoplexy, enteritis, and hydropsy were bigger killers of the elderly, heart attacks are not a twentieth-century product. But, as we have seen, French geriatrics bore scant relation to actual causes of death, save where organic atrophy was involved. (*Mouvement de la population,* 1859-60. Unfortunately causes of death were not recorded again for the whole population until the mid-1920s, because doctors were unwilling to report.) Furthermore British nineteenth-century studies dealt seriously with heart lesion, long before serious French interest. Bernard Muller, *Le Coeur Vasculaire chez le Vieillard* (Thèse présenté à la Faculté de Médecine de Lyon, 1938).
29. Millot, *Gérocomie,* pp.360ff; Rauzier, *Traité des maladies des vieillards* (Paris, 1909), p.27, noted that the heart 'resists best' of all the organs.
30. Charcot also noted frequent ruptures of the heart, without following this up.
31. O. Josué, *La Séminologie cardiaque actuelle* (Paris, 1914); though see also Boy-Tessier, *Old Age,* in T.L. Stedman, *Twentieth-Century Practice* (New York, 1897), XII.
32. Corderet, *Preuves de l'insénéscence du sens intime de l'homme et conséquences physiologiques de cette vérité* (Montpellier, 1844), p.90 and *passim,* M. Chauffard, 'De la Situation de l'Enseignement médical en France,' *Revue des deux mondes* (1878), pp.124-66.
33. S.A. Turck, *De la Vieillesse étudiée comme maladie* (Paris, 1854).
34. Fernand Papillon, 'Les Régénérations et les greffes animales,' *Revue des deux mondes* (1872), pp.949-67.
35. P. Flourens, *De la longévité humaine* (Paris, 1854), p.33 and *passim.*
36. Boy-Tessier, *Old Age,* XII, p.463; see also Reveillé-Parise, *Traité,* p.85. This view persisted as late as 1940 among self-professed followers of Hipprocrates. See Paul Carton, *Le Guide de le Vieillesse* (Paris, 1851), *passim.*
37. Dr Pétron, *L'Ami de l'homme* (Paris, 1853), I, p.208; Charles Vidal, *Le Vieillard* (Paris, 1924), p.103.
38. Millot, *Gérocomie,* p.288; R. de Grailly and H. Destrem, *Physiologie générale, diététique et comportement de la Vieillesse* (Paris, 1953), p.233.
39. Lest this seem purely male bias, see the widely sold book by Dr Anna Fischer on the post-menopausal women: 'Then woman has no more reason to exist, since the principal function of her life has ended.' Anna Fischer, *La Femme, Médecine au Foyer* (Paris, 1905).
40. A. Lorand, *La Vieillesse, Moyens de la prévenir et de la combattre* (Paris, 1911).
41. O. Josué, *Séminologie, passim,* and *Traité de l'Artério-sclerose* (Paris, 1909), p.122; Flourens, *Longevité, passim.*
42. Alex Comfort, *The Biology of Senescence* (New York, 1956), p.5; A. Sabatier, *Essai sur la Vie et la Mort* (Paris, 1892).
43. Boy-Tessier, *Age,* p.485.
44. Emile Demange, *Etude clinique et anatomo-pathologique sur la vieillesse* (Paris, 1886), pp.24, 49ff.
45. Léri, *Cerveau,* p.3.
46. A. Létienne, 'De la sénilité,' *La Presse médicale* (1906), pp.65-6.
47. Rauzier, *Traité, passim,* suffered similarly in the main twentieth-century text on geriatrics. Beginning with the plea that old age not be regarded as a disease, as distinct from diseases that occurred in old age, he was soon saying that the elderly must be treated as if they were sick and finally, after his dismal contemplation of the major causes of death and the lack of much but

palliative therapy, concluded that old age itself was a major malady.

Again, the Paris school was not undisputed, though by now its approach spread to schools and research hospitals all over France. From Lyons, Pic and Bonnamour took a slightly different approach. Dealing with wealthier patients — hence a recommendation of Mediterranean trips for old people suffering from lung problems — instead of the very poor, the Lyons faculty was more interested in therapy and diagnosis. Pic and Bonnamour stressed use of the electro-cardiogram more heavily than did Rauzier; they discussed medicines to tone the heart and reduce hypertension; they noted with approval the German practice of regular small doses of digitalis as a preventative. But (save for a mild bow to testicular liquid in cases of constipation, followed by a quick note that this was not general practice) they took no interest in hormonal treatments, which were also receiving attention in Germany. Their approach was not pathological, for the focus was on specific diseases; but the therapeutic arsenal was not unusual and there was extreme resistance, save in the case of the digitalis suggestion, to innovation. Above all, while arguing with the Paris school on organic specifics, Pic and Bonnamour shared the basic pessimism with regard to much more than palliative treatment for most of the diseases of old age. Adrien Pic and S. Bonnamour, *Précis des Maladies des vieillards* (Paris, 1912).

48. Léri, *Cerveau*, p.137.
49. Boy-Tessier, *Age;* Pic and Bonnamour, *Précis.*
50. Dr Burhureaux, *Un Danger social: la Purgation* (Paris, 1908), attacked the common practice of purging to deal with any disease, especially for the elderly; he even advised against laxatives as too tiring for many patients.
51. See also Pic and Bonnamour, *Précis,* who urged the operability of normal old patients.
52. Rauzier, *Traité,* p.559; see also Pic and Bonnamour, *Précis.*
53. Brown-Séquard, 'Exposé des effets produits chez l'homme par des injections souscutanées d'un suc rétiré des testicules d'animaux,' *Archives de Physiologie,* (1890), pp.1-25.
54. It was also Brown-Séquard who in 1887 recommended oxygen treatments for fatigue in the elderly, but the first small unit was set up only in 1910 and extensive medical research had to await Binet in the 1940s. Pierre Vachet, *Vivre Vieux, rester jeune* (Paris, 1958).
55. Rauzier, *Traité,* p.112; it was true, of course, that before the isolation of pure hormones many solutions of extracts had only brief effects, but despite variability few were worthless.
56. Jean Finot, *La Philosophie de longévité* (Paris, 1900), p.102; Elie Metchnikoff, *Etudes sur la nature humaine* (Paris, 1903).
57. J. Grasset, *La Fin de la vie* (La Chapelle-Montligeon, 1903), p.20.
58. J. Delay and S. Brion, *Les Démences tardives* (Paris, 1962), pp.29ff.
59. S. Gujetant, *Le Médecin de l'âge de retour et de la vieillesse* (Paris, 1836), p.86 and *passim.*
60. See also Edouard Auber, *Hygiène des femmes nerveuses* (Paris, 1844), pp.474ff; only V. Raymond advised against bleeding on grounds that menstrual blood was not impure and so its cessation was not dangerous: *Etude hygièniques sur la santé, la beauté et la bonheur des femmes* (Paris, 1841), pp.61-2.
61. Charles Vinoy, *La Ménopause,* (Paris, nd.), pp.107ff.
62. Burhureaux, *Danger.*
63. Pétron, *Ami,* II, pp.481, 485.
64. *Gazette de Santé,* 1905; *Gazette de la Médecine,* 1861.
65. Burhureaux, *Danger.*
66. Ferran, *Médecine de la Vieillesse* (Paris, 1900), *passim.*

67. *Gazette Médicale des familles,* 1872; *Journal de médecine,* 1952; J. P. Nazier, *Le Rhumatisme* (Paris, 1953).
68. Anon., *Le Secret de longue vie* (Paris, 1873), *passim.*
69. *Statistique de la France, Mouvement de la population,* 1870-1899; *Statistique de la France, Statistique annuelle de institutions d'assistance,* 1899ff. For causes of death 1926ff see *Mouvement de la Population; Causes de decès:* definitions have varied and figures are invoked only to indicate general trends.
70. Burhureaux, *Danger.*
71. Pic and Bonnamour, *Précis;* Durand-Fardel, *Traité.*
72. *Statistique de la France, Mouvement de la population,* 1962.
73. P. Bastai and G. C. Dogliotti, *Physiopathologie de la Vieillesse* (Paris, 1938); Nathan Shock, *Bibliography of Geriatrics and Gerontology* (Chicago, 1963).
74. A. Bréton and C. Dehorter-Duez, 'L'Oeil dans la vieillesse,' *Echo médical du Nord* (1942), pp.481-8.
75. Léon Binet and Francois Bourlière (eds.), *Précis de Gérontologie* (Paris, 1955).
76. Muller, *Coeur, passim.*
77. Vidal, *Vieillard,* p.144 and *passim.*
78. *Guérir,* 1936.
79. Aélina Gaboriau, *Les Trois âges de la femme* (Paris, 1923), p.179.
80. J. Kramerz, *Contribution à l'étude du traitement des accidents de la ménopause* (Thèse pour le doctorat, Paris, 1931); Georges Mondin, *La Ménopause* (Thèse pour le doctorat en médicine, Bordeaux, 1931); E. Doray, *Gynécologie* (Paris, 1933); Bernard Sommillon, *Action des Extraits placantaires sur les troubles de la ménopause* (Paris, 1932); H. Vignes, *Physiologie gynécologique* (Paris, 1929).
81. E. Juster, *La Ménopause* (Paris, 1952).
82. *Formulaire Ostier: Vade mecum de médecine pratique* (Paris, 1937).
83. Celos and Wagner, *Vie et Santé* (Paris, 1934), I, pp.271-2.
84. Charles Richet, *Savoir Rester Jeune* (Paris, 1950); *Troisième Age,* 1957.
85. Richet, *Savoir,* p.173 and *passim.*
86. S. Delmond, *Harmonie de la santé* (Angers, 1948), p.170 and *passim.*
87. *Cri du retraité,* 1934-36; *Guérir,* 1932.
88. L.H. Goizet, *Ne Jamais vieillir* (Paris, 1931).
89. Jacques Marcireau, *L'Art de vivre très vieux* (Paris, 1947).
90. *Gazette médicale de France,* 1951.
91. *Vieillesse heureuse,* 1957.
92. *Guérir,* 1932, Binet and Bourlière, *Précis.*
93. Vignes, *Physiologie;* Pol Boutin, *A Propos de quelques phénomènes de dégénérescence dans les cellules en activité karyo kinetique* (Paris, 1896); E. Gley, *Quatre Leçons sur les sécretions internes* (Paris, 1921); Léopold Lévi, 'Glandes à sécretion interne,' *Revue d'Anthropologie* (1918).
94. Alexis Carrel, *L'Homme, cet inconnu* (Paris, 1935), p.219.
95. Alexis Carrel, *Jour après Jour* (Paris, 1956), p.104.
96. P. Lecomte de Nouy, *Méthodes physiques en biologie et médecine* (Paris, 1933) and *Le Temps et la vie* (Paris, 1936).
97. Serge Voronoff, *Les Sources de la vie* (Paris, 1933)
98. By 1930 he had conducted 475 operations, 236 on people 55 to 70; Serge Voronoff, *La Greffe testiculaire de singe à l'homme* (Paris, 1930).
99. Dartigues, 'Chirurgie génito-endocrienne,' in V. Pauchat, *La Pratique chirurgicale illustrée* (Paris, 1930).
100. Paul-Henri Paillou, *Victoires sur la mort* (Paris, 1947), p.121. Even earlier Emile Maupas, working in obscurity on plasma injections in Algiers, was totally ignored by the French medical profession, though he had considerable international reputation among biologists; Dr Saint-Pierre, *Prolonger la Vie* (Paris, 1948).
101. Henri Bouquet, *La Médecine du temps présent* (Paris, 1925), p.127; see also

Auguste Lumière, *Sénilité et rajeunissement* (Paris, 1932). Lacassagne, in *Vieillesse,* revived a different tradition in dealing with endocrinology; he accepted the findings but applied them to a philosophical discussion of the causes of aging, not to therapy, where he remained quite conventional except in his acceptance of American work on the importance of vitamin treatment.

102. Roger des Allées, *Défense de Vieillir* (Vienne, 1950), *passim.*

103. Richet, *Savoir.*

104. A. Bidon and E. Bidon, *Place aux Vieux* (Lyons, 1951), p.60.

105. Breton and C. Dehorter-Duez, 'Oeil,' pp.481ff; E. Houche, 'Réflexions sur le traitement des accidents vasculaires cérébraux chez le vieillard,' *Echo médical du Nord* (1954), pp.125-32; E. Houche and P. Fournies, 'Le Poumon du vieillard,' *Echo médical de Nord* (1954), p.111.

106. Binet and Bourlière, *Précis;* Leon Binet, 'Action thérapeutique du testérone chez les sujets agés,' *La Médecine* (1943), p.15; H. Destrem, 'La Pharmacologie de la vieillesse,' *Concours medical* (1954), p.2395; H. Destrem, 'A Propos des thérapeutiques de la sénéscence; association vitaminique acide nicotinique-thiamine,' *Semaine hospitalière* (1955), pp.209-22.

107. Yves Salembrier, *Chirurgie gérontologique* (Paris, 1957).

108. Henri Charbonnel, *Jeunes de 16 à 80 ans?* (Paris, 1954), p.64.

109. Léon Binet, *Biologie de la sénéscence* (Paris, 1956), pp.16ff; P. Baumgartner, *Les Consultations journalières en gérontologie* (Paris, 1968); Hugues Destrem, *A la conquête de la troisième age* (Paris, 1958).

110. Nazier, *Rhumatisme.*

111. Charles Nordmann, 'Le Rôle de la sécretion interne,' *Revue des deux mondes* (1920), pp.931-42.

112. *Guérir,* 1936; *Cri du Retraité,* 1938.

113. *Troisième age,* 1972. Even in the early 1960s this periodical, in its medical column, dealt with organic deterioration and with hygiene rather than with therapeutics; a change in tone developed with each succeeding year.

114. Bidon and Bidon, *Place,* pp.60ff.

115. *Troisième age,* 1965.

116. Binet and Bourlière, *Précis, passim.*

117. Shock, *Bibliography, passim;* see Baumgartner, *Consultations,* which offers sound advice but devotes most space to yet another clinical analysis of how and at what rate the senses and organs decline.

118. Caisse nationale de retraite des ouvriers du bâtiment et des travaux publics, *Réalités,* p.220.

119. For an overview, see Gerald Gruman, 'A History of Ideas about the Prolongation of Life,' American Philosophical Society *Transactions,* 56, Part 9, 1966, an interesting comment on current American practice, which must qualify any comparative belaboring of the French; see also, for a clear counterpart to French theory and practice, Lawrence Galton, *Don't Give Up on an Aging Parent* (New York, 1975), in which American doctors are taken to task also for unexamined assumptions.

4 OLD WOMEN, AND SOME OLD MEN

Older women were treated horribly in the popular culture of traditional society. It has already been stressed that widows past 45 were not expected to remarry in the villages, though a minority had enough defiance, or property, or even good looks to do so. At the more formal level of the published literature, older women were derided; even the grandmotherly role, though not ignored, was given scant prestige. Doctors long enhanced the popular culture, though this was primarily a function of being trapped by it. The eagerness with which alleviations of difficult menopause were adopted, through hormonal treatments, shows that the most salient feature of the medical outlook was eagerly escaped by many practitioners and practionees alike when a remedy was finally presented.

Yet the sex differential must be stressed, even if partially in summary or anticipation of the more general themes in a discussion of France's elderly. With a special set of attitudes persistently applied to their post-menopausal years, women were further burdened or blessed with unusual longevity. Their dilemma and their reaction to it, when men are used as a control group, form the subject of this chapter. Women not only improved their longevity record more rapidly than men but seem to have adapted better to old age, despite cultural hostility. If we can describe what happened better than we can explain it, the sex differential provides vital insight into aging and offers some tentative suggestions about how old people learned to improve their lot.

A woman in industrial society who lives to be twenty can expect to spend her last thirty years classified, or potentially classified, as old. Slightly more than a third of the French female population consists of women over 50. At age 70 there are now about 40 percent more old women than old men. From that point onward women die at a higher annual rate than men, but this is simply because more survive to that point in the first place, and, probably, because only exceptionally hardy men make it there at all. Despite rising death rates, women continue to outnumber men well past the centenarian landmark. In the period 1877-81 an adult woman had a life expectancy 8 percent higher than that of a man; at age 60, 7 percent. In the 1960s that variance had changed to 9 percent and 8 percent in the two categories.

One dismal but obvious statistic must be added: because of

superior longevity and lower age at initial marriage, women are far more likely to be widows than men are to be widowers. In 1851 9.4 percent of France's male population over 65 consisted of widowers, but 11.5 percent of the female population in the same age category were widows. The figures have worsened fairly steadily, with obvious qualifications for the 60-69 age group.[1]

Table 1: Widowage

Date	% of all women over 50 widows	% of all women over 70 widows
1851	38	68
1858	41	71
1891	43	69
1926	40 (male = 11% widowers)	72 (male = 23% widowers)
1926	41	72
1953	30	73
1963	29	74

In 1930 widows in their sixties were half as numerous (at 51 percent) of all married women in the same age group, while those aged 70-79 represented 89 percent of those women still married; since World War Two the percentages have been 39 and, again, 89.

The historical evolution of widowage figures results from three factors. First, a slight tendency in the population for increased differential in marriage age between man and woman; this automatically increases the probability of widowhood. In France the increase, of approximately a year and a half, explains 8 percent of the heightened widowhood over 50. More important by far is simply the rising rate of marriage. By the 1960s still 10 percent of all women over 50 had not married — a percentage twice as high as in Britain and most other industrial countries. But a century before, 23 percent of all older women were spinsters. Rapidly rising marriage rates have automatically increased the chance of widowhood. (They in fact explain approximately 50 percent of the rate over age 50.) Yet the growing disparity between male and female longevity is a still more obvious factor. Women gained over men in survival past fifty at a remarkable rate until the 1950s; thereafter, male survival improvement actually exceeded that of females for the 50-70 age period. But after 70 it is still all downhill for males, and the percentage of widowage faithfully reflects the comparative trend.

Women live longer. They are abused in culture, or have been until very recently. They have been scorned by doctors. They are far more likely than men to suffer the death of a spouse. And an additional obvious factor, less easily quantified than widowhood but related and no less real: they are far less well provided for materially. Men often recognized the demographic facts. They fought, in the working class particularly, more for provision for their wives than for their own pensions. The same held true in Germany, where 80 percent of all German workers in the 1920s bought private life or burial insurance — to assure an honorable ceremony but primarily to relieve their wives, spending some 30 percent more than on personal health insurance, which ironically might have been just as useful even to the women involved. Middle-class people, expecting death less early, reversed the pattern, insuring health and property primarily.[2] French workers struggled to obtain 50 percent pension levels for their wives, as we have seen. But the situation of older women could be desperate. In the early part of the twentieth century actual increases in percentages of women in the work force above 65 suggested the problem of widows, who needed new income, plus the necessity for single women to hang on to employment. A disproportionate number of women moved to the countryside,[3] in a pattern that still persists, seeking familial aid but above all, lower costs. A disproportionate number of women had to live with relatives, often against their own desire.[4] By the 1920s, as we have seen, a disproportionate number entered institutions for the aged. While not involving a vast group, this entry constituted a basic defiance of traditional female revulsion against being handled by outsiders. If widowed, the chances of remarriage as an economic and possibly emotional protection remained nil. Scorned by traditional culture, older women found rates of remarriage declining *per capita* well into the present century. In the period 1911-19, two times as many men 50-59 married as did women, despite the fact that there were fewer of them around. Marriages by the elderly declined generally in the later nineteenth century; between 1856 and 1906 the number of men marrying after 50 dropped 36 percent *per capita*, that of women 34 percent. But the percentage of women marrying at this 'great age' stayed at roughly 12 percent of the male rate. And virtually no women over 60 married in a given year until the last few decades. Culture was easily self-fulfilling in its pronouncements. Old women, defined as old at an early age, were useless, unmarriagable, impoverished, lucky

to get a job and forced to flee to the countryside if they could not
survive otherwise.

But survive they did. Their superior longevity cannot be explained by
a tale of undiluted despair. One more statistical offering sets up the
analytical problem: Men suffer horrendously when widowers, and their
suffering has increased with growing emotional dependence on ties with
their spouse. In 1876 the annual rate of death (percentage per population
category over 60) was 4.3 for bachelors over 65, 3.1 for married men,
but 6.4 for widowers. (A married man, in other words, was less than
fifty percent as likely to die as a widower of identical age.) Women
in the same year showed no distinction between spinsters and widows;
married women benefited from their state, but only at a 23 percent
rate compared to their sisters, in contrast to the 35 percent rate of
married men over bachelors and the 51 percent over widowers. In 1963
bachelors over 65 had gained on widowers, dying at a rate of only
5 percent more per year; but married men were still dying at a rate
53 percent under that of widowers. Men simply needed, and need, to
be married to maximize their longevity. Women may have developed
increasing emotional commitment to marriage, but it does not show
up in reactions to widowhood. In the years 1855-7 spinsters were
27 percent less likely to die than widows (and married women
87 percent) in the age category over 60. Evolution has been steady
since; by 1963 widows and spinsters over 60 had the same per
annum mortality rates, and widows were actually outliving
spinsters after age 70. Married women still preserved an advantage
over both groups, but only with 19 percent less chance of annual
death. If more older women were likely to be married, in the recent
stages of modernization, far fewer were likely to benefit through
special longevity.

Here is a case of adaptation to the realities of industrial life
characteristic of women's aging generally. Faced with far greater
probability of a spouse's death, and still far less ability to remarry
in later years, women simply refuse to be as demonstrably bothered.
Here is one reflection, and possibly an active cause, of greater
longevity. Retirement also creates fewer pangs. Women in France,
as elsewhere, increasingly work outside the home after marriage
and into middle age.[5] The spinsters who must work simply to
survive no longer dominate the statistics. They may suffer still,
particularly as retirement with mediocre pensions is forced upon
them — female workers certainly share their class culture in this
regard[6] — but they are buried now in the more general behavior

of their sex. Women retire earlier than men, by about eight years; they leave their job, in other words, at age 50-55. Their reason for work, the need to supplement family income in its building stage, is done. Past fifty they long have manifested less interest in work, greater likelihood of absenteeism and illness,[7] than men could afford. Hence retirement remains far less of a jolt. Contemporary observers note that women, normally committed to house-keeping even when formally employed, benefit from their ability to continue a major part of their routine. If retired they feel less functionless than men. The most mundane tasks, from which many younger women legitimately seek liberation, prove a solace in later years. Housework, apparently, beats fishing.

Traditionalism is thus a guiding factor in the female adaptation to old age, the result of a benign circle. Acclimated culturally to widowhood, rarely fully devoted to a job, women adjust to old age; a result is the increasing advantage over men in living into advanced years. And if schoolgirls reflect past culture in the inability to contemplate life after menopause, society overall accepts the older woman. Doctors proclaim her vitality, if in part because they will earn good money trying to preserve it. Cosmeticians do so with even greater fervor.

And here we enter the final area, difficult to pin down in so many aspects of women's history: traditionalists where tradition has proved beneficial, older women innovate where innovation is desirable. City dwellers here took a clear lead. Marriage rates for both sexes over 50 began to rise after 1906; women's rates remain far below men's (25 percent after 50) but their percentage increase, and particularly for the group over 60 — virtually hopeless matrimonially until the last four decades — has outstripped men's by some 58 percent. Cosmetic interest has spread steadily. The older woman seeks beauty, and the search spreads incessantly to lower income levels.[8] Face-lifting, initiated against formal medical advice over a century ago, is now enhanced by exercise, slimming, dyes, in sum a host of devices natural and artificial. In 1900 a German observer noted, with possible exaggeration, 'Today for most women there is no more old age.' And far earlier even Balzac had suggested that with hygiene and cosmetics women over forty could still remain 'competitive.'[9] Feeling better — particularly when doctors were able to aid in cases of menopausal difficulties — and looking better, older women made more rapid strides than men in defeating a culture of pessimism.

Women have a distinctive history of aging. They still face peculiar difficulties. Their very survival rate is one; a shakier material base another; the continued bias of society against the older female, indeed against her very appearance, yet a third. But they made do. Their success, carefully if often implicitly contrived, blends custom and innovation. They have no groups to represent them, in contrast even to the working class. They have had a singular lack of advocates yet perhaps they have not needed them. For if one slices the societal cake by sex rather than class, one begins to see the possibilities of change through individual initiative. This is where the elements of the elderly population have excelled, with women frequently leading the way.

Notes

1. *Statistique de la France, Mouvement général de la population,* 1856ff.
2. Sandra Coyner, 'Consumption Patterns in the German Lower-Middle Class,' *Journal of Social History* (1977).
3. See chapter V; the conclusion is based on census materials *(Statistique de la France)* since 1856.
4. See chapter V; the conclusion is based on *Listes nominatives* from three sample departments.
5. Patricia Branca, *Clio Muses* (London, 1976), *passim.*
6. Anne Lauran, *L'Age Scandaleux* (Paris, 1979), *passim.*
7. *Rapport de la Commission d'étude des problèmes de la vieillesse* (Paris, 1960), pp.43-7.
8. Janine Alaux, *101 Trucs pour vaincre le coup de vieux* (Paris, 1973).
9. M. Shram, *Des Anneés, oui; Vieillir, Non!* (Neuchatel, 1965).

5 WHERE THE ELDERLY LIVED AND LIVE

On the surface, nothing could be more prosaic than the question of the location of old people. In the years after World War Two one can even add to prosaica by citing the availability of bathrooms, refrigerators, and other basic elements of daily modern life. (Old people matched the general population in possession of such amenities, indeed, surpassing it in toilets, with a 95 percent ownership rate in 1962, by 37 percent.) A brief survey of residential patterns is called for because it offers the first definite indication of behavioral change and, relatedly, confirms overall class differences in behavior.

The first, fundamental statement is unsurprising and might seem to undermine any further inquiry. From the mid-nineteenth century onward, most old people lived in the same community where they had resided at age 20 or 30. And even where a change in residence occurred, it is not always clear what it means. To refine the statement of the basic conundrum, when we can show that a widow moved in with relatives, we do not always know what is indicated in terms of personal identity; that is, we cannot pretend to offer certainty about the function or status the old person held in her new residence. What follows is a mixture of very firm data combined with unabashed speculation about what the data mean.

For residential patterns changed with modernization, in two respects. First, a minority stream of out-migration from the cities soared, dwindled and then resumed, but on quite different bases from the original thrust. Second, within the communities where the elderly had spent their adult lives, a distinct change of relationship to grown children occurred, with more and more old people living independently.

Rural out-migration, that is transfer of location from the city with older age, is unsurprising in an early-urbanizing situation. Studies in the United States have shown an interesting minority of older immigrants who 'go home again' with retirement. The same phenomenon occurred within individual European countries. To determine this, *grosso modo,* French departments were divided into urban, i.e. 50 percent resident in cities, and rural. Life expectancy rates were established for each of the two sectors. Controls were also introduced for birth rates and particularly adult age structures. Rural departments predictably manifested a much higher percentage of older people as soon as urbanization began, because the young were the movers; this factor has been controlled for by age structure. The results nevertheless manifested a distinct if minority movement of people past 60 or 65 to the countryside, calculated by means of an adjusted assessment of census figures.[1]

Table 1: Ruralization of the Elderly

Date	% of Elderly in Rural Departments Above Levels Predictable from Mortality and Emigration Rates	% of People Over 65 who moved to the Countryside
1864	5	9
1882	7	12
1891	3	9
1906	3	8
1926	2	6
1926	1.8	5
1946-50	1.2	5
1962	7	11

The above table is stark and subject to all sorts of quibbling about detail, given the number of imprecise variables (notably probably out-migration rates of young adults) that had to be taken into account. It does indicate, however, a fascinating trend. And a vast number of people were involved. In 1882, 280,000 people had moved in their later years from city to countryside; in 1906, 304,000. The ensuing decline meant that in 1936 only 171,000 had moved. But absolute numbers rose after World War Two, to 247,000, and by 1962 they stood at 577,000.

Even in 1936, at the trough of elderly out-migration, a city such as Paris had 16 percent fewer males over 65 than the national average, and 27 percent fewer males over 70. Urban departments overall had 12 percent fewer elderly. Similarly in 1946, before the second shift to ruralization, 6 percent more rural departments had more than 17 percent of all inhabitants over age 60 than did urban, and 19 percent more had over 8 percent inhabitants over age 70. It seems that, fairly consistently, the minority of people who moved did so between age 60 and 70, though a smaller group moved a bit earlier (this latter figure involved a disproportionate number of women, as we shall see). In terms of uncontrolled statistics, that is figures not adjusted for mortality and other pleasant things, in 1946 specifically rural communes (much more precise as units than departments) had 12.7 percent inhabitants over 65 – 14 percent female, 11 percent male; urban communes had a 9.3 percent total, involving 8 percent of all males and 10.2 percent of all females. Overall, this constituted a distinct shift from the situation half a century earlier. In 1891 urban departments averaged 10.9 percent of the total population over 60, rural 14.0 percent. Paris exuded some revulsion for only 8.1 percent of its population was over 60 (national average, 12.5 percent); cities over 300,000, 8.8 percent; cities over 100,000, 9.4 percent; over 10,000, 9.5 percent; over 50,000, 10.8 percent – overall urban average 9.6 percent. Controlled for mortality and probable in-migration of young adults (based on census age structure) Paris and large cities generally (which the Parisian figures dominate given the size of the capital) were pouring out some 9 percent of all their elderly; cities of lesser size were remaining stable. But in 1967, as a final factual offering, people 65 and over of agricultural origin stood slightly under the national average, while those of urban origin exceeded it. Rural rates, in other words, were no longer reflecting rural roots.

Two questions arise from this terse statistical effort. First, what is the impact of concentration or non-concentration of the elderly? Second, what caused the chronological trends?

We are all aware that the industrialization-urbanization process produces villages crammed with old people. The young leave in vast disproportion to their numbers – in France this process affected demographic balance in both city and countryside by the 1850s and has continued steadily since. The results in terms of reduced village vitality have often been discussed, mirroring of course aspects of the conventional wisdom about the overall sterility of the aged. But note the problem suggested in terms of the elderly themselves. The undeniable imbalance between old and young in village and city raises a number of possible quandaries. Is an unusual concentration of elderly in a village salutary? One could argue that the loss of village dynamism, reflected in very personal terms through the departure of one's own children, creates a mournful atmosphere, a sort of unorganized public old age home. But possibly also, a concentration of old people is a good thing, allowing them mutual support and a commonality of interests. If so, the urban dispersion of elderly, less able to meet if only because of low statistical incidence in the population, could suggest real problems of self-identity. The difficulty the urban elderly, now numerically predominant if still underrepresented, express with regard to formation of recreational groups suggests that this might be a genuine dilemma. The feeling, emanating again particularly from the cities, that the 'young' do not appreciate or understand the 'old' might be in part a function of sheer lack of density.

Which leads logically to the second issue, the explanation of chronological patterns of out-migration from the cities. Three factors could have been involved in the initial wave of out-migration: (1) a belief that the countryside was healthier; (2) the necessity of cutting costs; (3) the desire to return to a familial atmosphere, particularly in times of early urbanization. Factors 2 and 3 are easily related; factor 1 is probably invalid but interesting.

Rural death rates for adults were higher than urban throughout the later nineteenth century. Life expectancy at age 50 in the 1860s was 9 months lower in rural departments than in urban. Paris had a worse record than the countryside in the 1860s but this may in part have been due to movement of the sickly to the reputed hospitals of the capital; otherwise the generalization is firm. And even in the Parisian case adult life expectancy dipped below the national average only until age 65; thereafter it was actually somewhat higher. By 1900, finally, Parisian longevity from 50 had risen 2 percent above the national average. One can of course argue that in the cities hosts of people died before reaching old age, that the phenomenon referred to is simply a matter of the fittests' survival. But this is, first, statistically incorrect; even from birth or from age twenty longevity was lower in the countryside. This follows from poor rural nutrition, the migration of the most vigorous elements to the cities, and so on. And second, even if correct the argument would not necessarily influence decisions to leave the city for one's final years.

Yet people did leave. Individuals may have been influenced by medical advice on the healthiness of the countryside. Far more may on their own have judged the city impure. But the minority out-migration to rural regions was primarily lower-class and based on material and familial considerations.

Nineteenth-century out-migration assumed one of two forms, sometimes combinable. It was either short-distance, designed to take advantage of lower rural prices (and, possibly, familial ties) or longer-distance, based on familial origins (although obviously compatible with the desire to seek lower prices). Well into the twentieth century the Parisian *banlieue* and nearby departments such as the Eure had a disproportionate number of elderly. Until 1926, the Eure, about 60 kilometers from Paris at its nearest points, contained large numbers of old people who had moved out from the metropolis.[2] Within the Seine department, in 1911, Paris had but 3.0 percent of its population over 65 (national average for cities generally 6.1 percent) but the *banlieue,* much of it still semi-rural, had 6.3 percent.

Overall, then, out-migration seems to have been relatively short-distance in the later nineteenth century and into the twentieth. This reflects the fact that original migration had also often been of short distance, so that in going back, say, to the Eure one was returning to a known area in which relatives might be present. More likely, however, the short distance followed from a desire to stay within hail of relatives in the city while taking advantage of lower rural or small-town prices.

Within this framework, several patterns emerge clearly. First, the vast majority of out-migrants was working-class. This follows of course from material pressures; it also suggests the need to play down perceived health benefits. Three sample studies, from Avignon in the Vaucluse, Gisors in the Eure, and the 18th arrondissement of Paris,[3] produce identical conclusions. Using occupation as a rough class designation almost no middle-class people left the city after age 55; approximately 12 percent of artisans, factory workers, and laborers did so. The same conclusion emerges from studies of villages in the Eure and the Vaucluse in the same period; older in-migrants, and there were few who were not old, listed working-class backgrounds almost without exception. These people, arranging their lives before mass retirement or pension benefits, moved as a result of material necessity. Women went back to the countryside more frequently than men. As they survived longer, this is no surprise, but even controlling for this factor their return rate between 1860 and 1906 was 3 percent higher than the male. This can be confirmed impressionistically from departments near major cities, such as the Eure, and from the *banlieue* of the Seine. Widows were far more likely to return to the countryside than women in general, again the result of material compulsion. Tragically, this overall pattern did not send older women back to relatives. Departments such as the Finistère, which exported hordes of women to Paris as servants, actually had more old men than old women, again throughout the century beginning around 1860. Women either adapted better to the urban environment from the rainy Breton area; or were forced to keep working as servants or otherwise rather than risk return; or left Paris but for a closer, more readily-afforded journey to a nearby village. The Vaucluse, similarly, saw few widows residing in villages who had not been there during their entire lives; the department was simply too far from major urban centers to be relevant. Widowers, it might be noted, did not emigrate from the cities disproportionately; their resources were more adequate, and while some had to leave the percentage was at the level of the national average for the out-migration of the elderly.

But if material compulsion looms largest as the explanation for the first wave of bucolic fever among the elderly, family ties were also sought. In the two heavily rural departments studied the elderly chose to move to the village from which the wife had originated; almost never did they go to the village of the male's provenance or to an unfamiliar village. The choice followed from working-class culture. The male, surprised he had survived so long, was primarily concerned about protecting his wife. Working-class patterns of family ties based on the female networks of relatives may have encouraged this behavior as well. But the choice could involve tragedy. The male, unknown in the village and disoriented by cessation of work, might precipitate his own demise or senility. Few of the male migrants to villages worked. Few couples lived directly with relatives. In Vaucluse villages, at least, few even had relatives identifiable by name still resident in the area. In other words, Mme Magon née Fauget may well have come from the village, or a nearby village, to which she and her husband returned in their later years (most typically from Marseilles), but the Faugets had all decided to leave or had died off. There was no Fauget or née Fauget down the street or in the village at all. Again, family links may have been hoped for but they were rarely found. The advantage of the countryside remained primarily a matter of lower cost of living, and even here disappointment may have been frequent.

And this explains of course the evolution of out-migration. As workers obtained more adequate pensions they sought to remain in the city. Family ties, even if only a pipe-dream, became totally urban as well. So, by 1936, virtually no out-migration at all. (The small residue, however, still followed the old patterns, predominantly working-class seeking the wife's village.) However exiguous, survival was now possible in the city. One's children were there. The countryside lost its charm.

But in this same period the middle class began to discover rural

splendor. Advertisements in magazines directed at state retirees
constantly pushed the rural house with small garden attached. Doctors
were persistently urging the advantages of life in the countryside. In the
1930s, with pensions still modest even for the middle class and with
inflation followed by depression creating the urgent need to continue
work if possible, few could actually go rural. Hence the decline in
total out-migration. But after 1950 the situation changed. Early
industrial rates of out-migration were restored, but on a quite different
basis.

Movement was now predominantly middle-class, not linked to places
of origin, and disproportionately directed toward the sun and health.
The numbers of migrants were substantial. They headed to departments
such as the Vaucluse, which offer almost perpetual sun and boast a
number of mountain villages reputed for their longevity proclivities.
In 1946 the Vaucluse had but 1 percent over the national average of
elderly people, quite low for a rural department. But by 1962 it was
a whopping 6 percent above. Studies of 17 villages indicate up to
51 percent of all resident elderly were in-migrants who arrived after
60 years of age. Correspondingly departments closest to urban
centers are no longer special havens; the Eure for example, and the
Parisian *banlieue* (now chopped up into various departments to divide
Communist electoral strength) are actually under the national average
for percentage of population over 65, again controlled for mortality
and probable in-migration of younger people.

Seventy percent of all Parisian residents over 65 profess the desire
to remain in Paris.[4] This may suggest some frustration, because there
is no chance for most of the remaining 30 percent to get out. But it
reflects the massive fact: most people, particularly in the lower classes,
want to stay where they have always stayed. Women still
disproportionately leave the city; one cannot neglect either familial
ties or the brute force of inadequate pensions and lack of jobs.
Nevertheless, the scenario has changed almost completely.

One goes to the Vaucluse (or the Alpes-Maritimes, which also
reflects a massive disproportion of older residents). The village of
Saint-Saturnin, reputed for its healthiness, contained in 1962 a few
women (6 percent of those over 65) born in or near the village and
returned from other places (mostly Paris, Lyons, or Marseilles). But
its older immigrant population is composed primarily of couples with
no previous ties to the area. As in the village of Saint Roman de
Malegarde, the married couples live alone with their spouse. More are
from Marseilles (about 100 kilometers distant) than from any other

city and visits from relatives in the city are frequent. These people are retired, though they often do some farming as a pastime and an income supplement. Their presence plus that of older farmers produces an overwhelming percentage — up to 75 percent — over 60 in the total adult population. Most of the farmers are retired as well. But there is little interaction. The city folk patronize different cafés, profess (in interviews undertaken) only nodding acquaintance (and this in the morning, not in cafés) with the local elderly.

Material necessity thus drove people out of the city in the early stages of French industrialization. They may have sought more than material solace, but it is doubtful that they found it. Families, as well as jobs, simply were not available. This supports the hypothesis that industrialization initially worsened the lot of the old. But change came. The working class, with family networks now established in the city, decided to stay. They could afford to, even though their pension situation was hardly encouraging. But material compulsion had yielded, as prime causation, to family ties and the sheer joy of staying in the apartment one had always lived in. For significant elements of the middle class the pattern differed. They sought the sun. They purchased rural retreats of a certain elegance. They were justly confident that their families could visit them, by car, taking advantage most recently of the autoroute network. But their nest was built less on previous eggs than on a desire to live as a couple, to make new friends and above all to enjoy a change of scene.

The result, demographically, is that the Parisian area, heavily working-class, now enjoys or suffers from a percentage of elderly above the national average. So, of course, do most rural areas. Growing centers of industry offer the exception, which produces the national average. The general rule is this: most older people want to stay where or near where they were born, which is usually now in a city. A divergent minority of predominantly middle-class types seeks an alternative.

What, however, of the fate of the majority, who did not wish or found it impossible to undertake a major move? In 1962, 33 percent more of all people not residing in the countryside were working than was the case in villages. One fact, then, is again the class distinctions that persist in old age, involving work and material need. The latter may be predominant, but personality types should not be disregarded even as class advantage is retained. The rural-bound may simply be better able to cope with leisure than the urban, and make their choice on that basis. This statement can of course be totally reversed in implication with no change of data: the rural bound are lazier than the urban who find their purpose in life still wrapped up in some retention of a work role.

The urban elderly are now less likely to enjoy prolonged longevity than the rural. This reflects major changes in the agricultural standard of living. It may provide quite rational causation among people able to afford displacement; certainly it mirrors the fact that unusually healthy (and socially advantaged) people are now moving to rural regions, in contrast to the situation a century ago. Rural life expectancy was, as of 1962, 7 percent above urban, using age 50 as a base. The transition occurred between the wars, just as the residential switch began to take place. In 1935-37 rural males had a death rate 8 percent under the national average per annum, rural females 10 percent.

One other point in our backdrop. The number of surviving children, for people aged 65 and over, has altered. In 1901 the average French male over 60, rural or urban, had 1.2 surviving children.[5] Despite falling birth rates, by the 1930s the figure had risen. Elderly males had 8 percent more surviving children than in 1911, whether married, widowed or divorced. The number of elderly with large families (over 3 children) had dropped, but that with 1-2 children had risen more than enough to compensate. This resulted from higher marriage rates from the late nineteenth century onward and, to a lesser extent, from decreased mortality (i.e. one's child was more likely to survive). Here was a potent force in residential patterns, particularly for old people in the working class who made their full transition to urbanism precisely in this period and initially on the basis of ties, financial and emotional, with their urban children.

Where, then, did the elderly live and in what circumstances? In the countryside at present as in the nineteenth century, the majority of married couples officially live in discrete households, with the male listed as household head. Rarely are children present under the same roof — in only 4 percent of the cases in the Eure, 3 percent in the Vaucluse in predominantly agricultural villages. French officials, including census-takers, love to take this as a sign of continued activity and social integration. However, many of the 'rurals' were never farmers at all, but are immigrants — in the Vaucluse over 50 percent list no previous rural profession — and have no intention of starting to sow and reap in their old age. They simply own their private dwelling. There is, however, a historic pattern of residence for agricultural families where one spouse has died. Males continue to be listed as family heads, which obviously reflects census-takers'

perceptions but perhaps some reality as well. More definite is the fact
that, in virtually all the agricultural households sampled, they lived
with sons; only 20 percent, in 1936, lived with daughters. The minority
had in essence either abandoned their basic property to their sons, or
their sons had moved away — tiring of waiting for the old man to give
over — or they had no sons in the first place. If listed as agricultural
laborers, they often even gave over the title 'chef de famille' to the
son-in-law.

Older widows form a more important case. Even in 1962, despite
the switch in migration patterns, women were 7 percent more likely
than men to live in the countryside. In the villages only 11 percent
of women over 65 lived alone. The rest lived with relatives; this
percentage persisted from 1936 to 1962. But, overwhelmingly, older
women lived with daughters. In the Vaucluse in 1946, 53 percent of
all women over 65 who had been married lived with daughters (almost
all the rest living with spouse). The rural pattern, reflecting
predominantly people who had lived their entire lives in the countryside but picking up some immigrants as well, was and is preponderantly
familial. Preference goes to living with spouse, but failing that one
seeks out a child. Males, still commonly property-owners and often
capable of some productive work, head for sons. Women, capable
of productive work but also natural baby-sitters, head for daughters.
This is viewed as immutable by in-laws. Sons-in-law find no reason to
take in their wife's father, for he offers them more trouble than
work, and characteristically no property. Daughters-in-law resist
the burden and emotional rivalry of their husband's mother. Rare
are the variations of this theme. And historical evolution has been
extremely slight.

The same does not hold true for cities. All of the urban samplings
produce comparable results. We can once more discount significant
institutionalization. The slight increase in entry to the *hospices* in
the 1920s has been noted. Figures for asylums and other possibly
convenient places to tuck old people away are miniscule; though
not age-specific, they would amount to less than 1 percent of the
population over 65 per year, since the 1920s, even if all were in this age
category. In 1951 of all people who died between age 60 and 70,
0.5 percent were in a retirement home, 1.3 percent in a state
institution other than a *hospice,* 2.9 percent in a *hospice* — a
total of 5 percent at the outside. Seventy-four percent died at
home, the rest on the street or in a public place. The conclusion
seems inescapable: the elderly in France have a home, a fact which

has not notably altered with urbanization.

But what home? Here we encounter significant change. In the twentieth century far more older people have maintained independent residence, as couples particularly; and since World War Two we know from polling data that this is precisely what they wish. A city such as Avignon, where data can be traced from 1856 to 1962, shows a vast increase of retirees — to the tune of 70 percent of all people over 65 in the past century. But retirement means independence; ironically it was when most artisans and small shopkeepers had or wanted to continue work that they lived with younger relatives. The dividing point occurred in the early 1930s, and without claiming absolute precision we must characterize the situation before and after.

Before, in what was essentially an early industrial framework for older people, most urban elderly worked. This was particularly true for women. We have already established this in terms of occupational data; we can now add the residential fact: those women with ties or hopes wrapped up in rural aspirations simply left, and many men did as well. But if one continued work in the city the common practice was to live with a relative, often an adult child. Income would not suffice otherwise; care was needed that would not be provided unless one had spouse or child for aid; yet probably the adult child had scant motivation to take the parent in without some contribution to income. This recalls the rural pattern which still persists. But there was a major difference. Particularly in working-class families, males as well as females, if deprived of spouse, lived with the eldest daughter.[6] There was no male preference for living with a son, because the urban proletariat had no property to transmit and no particular economic advantage in living with a son. Care, and perhaps love, was what was being sought, and the result was a major shift in residential preference.

By 1936, in the two cities and one Parisian district examined, this first change was supplemented. Given pensions and more attention to retirement, far more people lived alone in their older years — 85 percent in Avignon, 78 percent in Paris' 18th arrondissement. Of the Avignon figure 35 percent who were married still, and 50 percent of the unmarried, including widows particularly, lived within three blocks of a child — almost invariably a daughter. (In Avignon, of all those living near a child, 79 percent lived near a daughter.) Fifteen percent of the urban elderly lived *with* a child, again most commonly with a daughter. (About half in the cities wished this were not necessary.) Finally, even if employed and even if male, only a small minority (17 percent living with children were listed as heads) of household. Here of course is another census-takers' image, but perhaps more was involved. The urban old did not wish to live with their children, and if they did they had surrendered control. Well over half of all widows and widowers did not do this. The middle class led the way, given economic advantage – only 5 percent of all *rentiers* for example lived with children. Groupings of single old people, such as three sisters all over 65, were more common, most of them usually working. Yet, in Gisors twice, in the 1930s, and in Avignon in one case, families embraced both husband's and wife's mother (in two cases in a three-room flat); the emotional tension inferrable passes assessment.

Aberrations aside, the urban **pattern** had become clear and it has persisted, bearing every indication of correspondence with the preferences of the elderly themselves (though somewhat less with those of their offspring, who feel anachronistic responsibilities toward their progenitors whom they judge by definition incapacitated).[7] The old prefer to live as couples. Failing this, they prefer to live alone though within reach of children. An interesting minority, with appropriate means, want to escape the city altogether. If they are forced, by economic pressure or disability, to live with children, they almost uniformly opt for a daughter if available. This reflects a distinct difference from rural patterns and, quite possibly, an additionally good reason not to be a daughter A serious cultural change, based on internal relationships of emotion as well as property, is involved here. But the larger trend is the desire and increasing practicability of not depending totally or directly on any offspring. Class enters in; urban workers are far more likely to live close to children than elderly in the middle class. Sex enters in for obvious demographic reasons; widows so vastly outnumber widowers that their choice of daughters for coresidence magnifies an earlier, rural tradition.

But the main points derived from the evaluation of residential patterns are twofold. First, an increasing urbanization of the elderly, modified in the last three decades by the bucolic, sun-seeking yearnings of the growing middle class. Second, and really encompassing the first point, growing independence. Relatives are not shunned, but reliance on them has steadily decreased. The out-migrants from the city, the workers who stay in the city, who indeed cherish their older home even though it is now far bigger than they need, are displaying a common impulse. They want to take care of themselves, while carefully hoping to preserve emotional contact with their children. In this process the husband-wife relationship has become increasingly important, though widows and the rarer widowers seek independence as well. This was a striving that emerged in the cities long before pension plans and majority retirement took wide hold. It was indeed a reason to work on — for either children did not provide adequate support or, more probably, the support was overladen with dependence — the small bedroom, the care for grandchildren, the patent deference to presumed senility. This became unacceptable by the early twentieth century, on the part of married couples. By the late 1930s the majority of widows and widowers were in a position to take the same stance.

Polls since World War Two indicate no nostalgia for the transitional urban period when life with adult children was often an economic necessity. Urbanization altered residential patterns and desires. Economic causation yielded to adaptation to the city — indeed a defiant desire to stay in the apartment one had won through such work.[8] Or, in a smaller but intriguing number of cases, it yielded to the quest for a strange rural environment. The hope was to grow older with one's mate. Living with children was a distinct second best, and living in an institution was a *pis aller*. Here is the first, and among the most concrete, indication that the old became bent on shaping their own lives.

Notes

1. National figures in this chapter are calculated from *Statistique générale, Mouvement général de la population*, 1856ff, and censuses, 1863ff.
2. *Listes nominatives, département de l'Eure*, series M.
3. *Listes nominatives, Archives départementales* of the Eure, the Seine, the Vaucluse. Series M.
4. Suzanne Pacaud and M.D. Lahalle, *Attitudes, Comportements, Opinions des personnes agées dans le cadre de la famille moderne* (Paris, 1969). See also Ministère de la construction, *Le logement des personnes agées* (Paris, 1969).
5. *Statistique de la France, Statistique des familles* (Paris, 1903).
6. See the pattern in Avignon 1856-1952, *Listes nominatives, Archives départementales de Vaucluse*, 6M, pp.49-70.
7. Pacaud and Lahalle, *Attitudes*.
8. *Idem*.

6 TOWARD A NEW STYLE OF LIFE

Changes and variations in the behavior of the elderly occurred and are occurring within the working class, among women, and in terms of residence. Change is often distressingly individual — *the* retired railroad worker refuses to do the same things as the next retired railroad worker, and so confounds social judgments save for the convenient but widely accepted ploy of saying that old people vary more than any other age group. We are not excluding variation, by individual or by class, but something a bit more elaborate can be attempted. The claim is that elements of the middle class, the elements who did not base their lives and self-identification on property ownership, pioneered a new approach to the question of what to do when old. They in fact form the clearest group to want and, sometimes, to have a certain notion of what to do with retirement.

Association has remained difficult. But even when retired functionaries profess themselves unable to link up with the little, personalized clubs that half of them profess to want, 60 percent said they had adapted quite well to retirement. [1] We will run into traditional culture still, but this chapter is an affirmation that old people can shape, and in recent decades have shaped, part of their destiny. An oddly nineteenth-century message, in some respects, but taking quite novel forms and basically defying the traditional culture of rocking chair for grandma and genealogy for gramps.

We might as well begin dramatically, claiming that behavior changed in the nineteenth century, the middle class in the lead, through unprovable but highly probable assertions. Hints already found in changing residence patterns can be expanded by examination of sex, work-pension relationships and retirement activities among the middle-class elderly.

It is probable that the middle-class elderly indulged increasingly in sex, which is why doctors shouted so loudly against it even in the later nineteenth century. (Though, as always, the hand of tradition makes many old people claim impotence or actually become impotent to the present day.) Statistics are of no avail here, for sex among the elderly does not conveniently produce offspring, not even bastards, on which we might base grand claims of a gerontological sexual revolution. One important set of figures might even seem to

go against us: during the nineteenth century marriage among widows
and widowers, bachelors and spinsters over 50 became less common
than in traditional society.

Table I:[2] Marriages of People over 50 per year, per 10,000 marriagable
in the age group

	Women	Men
1856-1865	31	129
1866-1875	38	110
1876-1885	23	87
1886-1895	21	77
1896-1905	17	75
1907-1910	19	83
1906-1913	19	83
1914-1919	18	76
1921-1925	25	128
1926-1930	24	119
1935-1937	29	140
1951	26	123

It would be a bit ridiculous to break these small figures down further
into the over-60s, but in fact apparently virtually no woman over 60
remarried (or married for the first time) until after 1906, when a growing
handful began to be recorded. Older men, true to stereotype, took
younger brides if they married at all (although the average man over
60 had a wife over 60 as well). But the point is that so few of them
married, a point brought out sharply by comparison with figures for
the Habsburg monarchy, Spain, and Italy as early as 1860, where a
far higher percentage of widows and widowers remarried than in France.[3]
With the growth of a larger and larger percentage of propertyless people,
both in countryside and city, the inducement to marry an older person
waned; as we have noted, this affected women particularly, for they
were more likely to be propertyless and, according to the pervasive
culture that is still with us, had fewer physical attractions to offer
than the older man. With urbanization it may have become more
difficult to meet suitable partners as well. Obviously this situation
began to change — indeed to change dramatically, on a statistical
basis — after World War One, which will correspond with the rest of
the story we have to tell. One obvious addition, for all classes, that

applies especially to the twentieth century: many old people live together without marriage, so that the woman will not lose pension or, later, social security rights. But for the later nineteenth century the figures tell a potentially tragic story of loneliness and indeed more probable death (for the remarried lived longer than the single) that should not be neglected.

These are figures for the whole population, however. It is impossible to improve upon them for the middle class specifically, but we need not assume that the upturn in remarriage rates was so late for this class, where property ownership was general and health likely to be superior in addition. The upturn definitely began in cities, with Paris in the lead; the urban mentality was first to develop new concepts of the advantages of marriage or remarriage at advanced age. And one further point, that affects groups beyond the middle class as well: with slowly improving longevity, marriages among the elderly were slightly less likely to be dissolved by death; hence despite lower remarriage rates, the percentage of widows and widowers in the population between 50 and 75 actually declined somewhat after 1880.

And this returns us to the larger point, about sex. Countless older married people in the nineteenth century undoubtedly abstained from sex after menopause or andropause; among them may have been middle-class folk who listened to their doctor. Doctors still report great confusion about whether sex is proper or safe after age 60 or so; hence, now that their own opinion has changed, their need to pour out advice reversing the nineteenth-century view: 'Old people, you can make love as your appetite dictates.'[4] But clearly many people realized this before the doctors did. The 1919 study of Armengaud suggested that a majority of upper-class Bordeaux businessmen kept mistresses, to the horror of their doctor who told them that they were killing themselves.[5] More common in all probability was the continuation of occasional love-making within marriage. Certainly women, for all their new difficulty in remarrying if widowed, or perhaps because of this, did their best. The interest in cosmetics to preserve the appearance of youth grew steadily, as a the volume of nineteenth-century advertisements indicates. Interest by both sexes, though probably particularly men, in advertisements for sexual tonics, follows the same pattern.

We can see the results of this new outlook clearly in the interwar period, and it amounts to a mini-revolution. Of course some older people indulged in sex before modern times; it was the Princess de

Metternich, in the early nineteenth century, who, when asked at 62 about sex for older people, told her interlocutor to wait twenty years, until she was old. But for the common people, some of whom began to limit births by increasing abstention even before menopause, it seems improbable that sex played much role in life after middle age, particularly in the case of women; popular attitudes certainly ridiculed the notion. But by the interwar period remarriage rates had risen sufficiently to produce the following possible equation for men over 50: given mortality rates of about 0.8 percent per year, for the whole group (obviously rising with each year of age) and the fact that only about 15 percent of all marriages in this age category were contracted by bachelors, roughly 50-70 percent of all surviving widowers were now remarrying over a ten-year period. (In 1956-62, in the 60-64 age group alone 3 percent of all widowers were remarrying annually.)[6]

These are approximate, perhaps dry statistics, and unfortunately not matched among widows, despite the increased remarriage rate at a lower level. The phenomenon can be fleshed out from the literature produced for the elderly themselves, starting between the wars. 'Widow, 57, with property, seeks retiree for family life.' 'Widow lady, 57 years, with a little property, gay, affectionate character, unable to live alone, wants retired gentleman, 60 to 65. . . to pass a happy old age.'[7] More selfishly: 'Man, 51, 9200 francs pension, wants marry women 35-45, with job, living in South, or in North Africa.' But another widower, 57 years old, citing his 12,000 franc pension, stressed that the woman he sought must be 'affectionate.' The *Cri du Retraité* began its marriage column only in 1928, but it was quickly overwhelmed with inquiries. A sign of the difficulty of older people meeting suitable partners, but also a sign that this difficulty was being overcome. And 'affection,' which can probably be taken to include occasional sex, played a major role in this development. Hence the doctors, still unconverted until after World War Two, raised more and more laments about the fatal incontinence of the elderly.

From an admittedly speculative area, let us pass to a seemingly more concrete one, which however conceals its own ambiguities. All the advice to the elderly, well into the twentieth century, urged against retirement. Most middle-class people, if only out of material necessity, seem to have agreed. We can suggest retirement rates by again comparing age groups in one census, allowing for the then prevailing mortality in that group, and then determining the percentage of those living reported working in a later census. The results are interesting, for the middle class both pioneered in retirement and did not; the evaluation depends on the group examined and what retirement means.

Table 2: Retirement Rates over Age 65

	% persisting at work		% disabled or retired	
1896-1906	*Male*	*Female*	*Male*	*Female*
Agricultural employers	59	56	41	44
Mine employers	11		89	
Manufacturers	34	44	66	56
Commerce, Banking	36	40	64	60
Liberal Professions	77	44	33	56
Employees, Workers	61	32	39	68
State Employees	5	44	95	56

Source: Ministère du commerce, *Recensement général de la population* 1896 and 1906. These are the first censuses where such figures are available. Mortality rates in the period were 0.9 percent for the 60-64 age group annually, 1.33 percent over 65. These tables should be compared with those in Chapter II for workers.

1901-1926				
Agricultural employers	54		46	
Mines	31		69	
Manufacturing	30	35	70	65
Transport	43		57	
Commerce	34	35	66	65
Professions	64		36	
White-collar workers				
Manufacturing	23		77	
Transport	4		96	
Commerce, banking	13	19	87	81
Liberal professions	64		36	
Public service	6		94	

Source: Censuses of 1901 and 1906. Same procedure; roughly the same mortality rates prevailed. This is the first census in which employees were isolated as a group.

Table 2: Retirement Rates over Age 65 (contd.)

1901-1926	% persisting at work		% disabled or retired	
	Male	*Female*	*Male*	*Female*
Employers	76		24	
Employees	5		95	
Workers	37		63	

Sources: Censuses of 1901 and 1926. Here a different procedure was used, because the 1911 census and to a degree the 1921 census do not provide valid evidence. The 40-44 age cohort was taken in 1901, reduced by average mortality over a 25-year period. The above figures refer to the percentage of the 65-69 age cohort in 1926, probably alive, still working.

1926-1936				
Employers	40		60	
Employees	24	18	76	82
Workers	22		78	

Sources: Censuses of 1926 and 1936. Here we revert to the earlier procedure, save that mortality rates are now down by about 15 percent (i.e. 0.9 percent per year for all age groups over 60), which heightens the obvious conclusion that the persistence rates reflect a smaller percentage of those living actually at work. In the 1936 census, for example, 44 percent of all people actually listed themselves as 'retired' after 65, the first time the category had been used.

Several points emerge from these figures. Females employed in middle-class occupations initially found it harder to retire than men, because their resources were slimmer; but far fewer were employed by age 50 in the first place. The immense figures for female clerks in 1906 reflect an influx of older women into jobs that were light and, perhaps, respectable enough for them to handle. By 1936, however, the contemporary pattern where women retire earlier than men had been established. Until after World War Two employers were less likely than not to retire at 65, by a slight margin, and members of the liberal professions decidedly less likely than not.[8] Doubtless many of these people followed the advice the manuals offered and reduced their level of activity, but some contact was kept with the job. More prosaically the figures denote the need/desire for farmers and shop-owners to stick to tasks that were not always onerous. On the other hand, except in the liberal professions, where a particular zeal for work developed, a near-majority of those surviving to 65 *did* retire; not surprisingly, this is a far higher percentage than among workers until after World War One; as we

have noted between 1901 and 1906, for example, only about
34 percent of all workers retired by 65. Among mine-owners and
manufacturers retirement had become normal by 1900; in some
companies it was mandatory. So retirement is a relevant concept
for the property-owning middle class, even if not yet a majority
phenomenon; even a surprisingly large minority of agricultural
employees retired. After World War Two the trend would become
stronger, with only 17 percent of all manufacturing employers, for
example, continuing work after 65.

But if ambiguity, or individual range of choice, dominates the
employer group, the employee group (captured even in 1896 by
the public service category) found retirement logical very early. And
this despite lower lifetime earnings than employers in many cases
and, definitely, smaller families: in 1911 34 percent of all employers
had one child or no children living, but 47 percent of all employees.
In fact, low birth rates may have been part of a life pattern designed
to allow savings that in turn would make retirement possible. It also
denoted little expectation of depending on a child in old age: one
would make one's own way in retirement.

White-collar workers were the first large group to develop formal
retirement concepts and apply them massively. At first glance, this
would appear a definite if perhaps implicit defiance against the
conventional advice that one should keep working. Yet in a curious
way it could follow from the basic culture, for those who associated
aging with deterioration and decay might easily claim repose as
essential for their final years. This we have seen in working-class
culture, and along with the impact of depression and union and
employer pressure it explains why workers had passed even
employees in retirement rates by 1936. In fact, however, the origins
of the white-collar lead in retirement were more accidental, or,
better, non-intentional, than cultural, in terms of their relationship
to old age, and the notion of retirement long remained less absolute
than it looks on paper, even census paper.

We can trace the history, admittedly, only through state pensioners,
who have left an abundant literature, including of course legislation
itself; but the general concepts undoubtedly apply to the white-collar
class as a whole. State pensions began with the military, in the
seventeenth century. The revolution of 1789 spread the concept,
and to some extent the practice, to certain civil employees, among
whom a series of private plans also proliferated during the first half
of the nineteenth century. Here was clear sign that some thought

was already being given to aging. These plans were regularized by a law of 1853, whose provisions were extended, during the next few decades, to teachers, postal workers, and so on, and it is this law that most clearly shows the need to dissociate pensions from retirement well into the present century.[9] In 1852 a grand total of 1,776 people were receiving pensions; in 1862, 10,995; in 1872, 29,395; in 1882, with a final breakthrough to some magnitude, 123,688. Pension plans inherently take time to have effect, if they are based on participant contributions; unless subsidized, it will be twenty-five years before they change retirement patterns significantly, and these pensions were almost entirely contributory. Equally important, because we have no intention of drifting into the incredibly complex history of pension legislation, the state did not intend the 1853 pension plan as a device for general retirement; the plan was not designed with any eye to the desirability, much less the consequences, of actual retirement. And the participants in the plans did not necessarily intend to retire either. There was immense desire to participate in the state plans; civil engineers, for example, long agitated for inclusion in the system. But from the participants' standpoing the plans were primarily: (1) a sign of prestige; (2) a guarantee of some protection for one's widow; and (3) possibly, provision of a certain range of choice for oneself if, in later years, one were disabled or attracted by other activities. But in none of this was there a collective notion of retirement or what to do with it.

The 1853 law stemmed from two motives on the part of the state. First, to regularize the many little plans then existing and give them sounder and wider actuarial footing. Second, to give the state the basis to fire incompetent employees at a certain age – an impulse which academicians will recognize in the present day. In fact, the state more often retained than fired old workers; teachers, for example, in short supply, were wont to complain around the turn of the century that they were kept on beyond their time. There was tension between a desire for choices (and an understandable wish to cash in on one's own contribution) and the reality of the state's intent. For although the government plan was compulsory for the employee, not until the 1920s did legislation make it obligatory for the state to pay pensions out at a definite age. Finally, in perhaps the most common pattern of all, the employee might be retired, only to return as an assistant – this helps explain the earliest census figures, which are thus clearly faulty. This had the great advantage for the state of providing experienced personnel at a lower pay scale. It had a certain advantage for the retiree in allowing him the chance to work less regularly while keeping contact with what had been his life. Lower pay might be resented, but it was not an active grievance save for those retirees whose pensions were so modest that they had to resort to manual labor. Overall, however, the pension scheme worked well in the nineteenth century because it often did *not* involve retirement (save where outright disability was present) and might allow a certain range of choice to the employee himself. We should not, then, be deluded by the census figures. The middle class was more united than the figures suggest around 1900; united in its division, that is. A large number retired, among proprietors but also functionaries and clerks; a large number worked, even if, as with the state functionaries, they did not appear as formally employed because of their 'auxiliary' status.

Primary stress, then, both for employers and employees, must be placed on the variety of situations, conditioned of course by the material and physical difficulties of old age but involving some personal choice as well. If there was an element of accident in the initial pension schemes, at least in relationship to actual old age activities and expectations, the very existence of the schemes helped develop a new consciousness of aging and even of certain rights attached to it. The middle class expected to live to old age. It was the first large class to prepare for this stage of life. Its interest in savings (and/or preservation of property in shop or farm), its growing participation in pension plans followed from this outlook. Aging might still mean decrepitude, although groups like professionals who kept working did not think so. But to get deeper into middle-class consciousness, admittedly evolving over time, two further questions: what happened when a group found its choice eliminated, with retirement made obligatory; and what did those people who retired, whether voluntarily or not, do with their lives?

The first question is easiest to tackle because it produced an abundance of debate, beginning shortly before World War One but cresting between the wars. The state's handling of pensions had one obvious disadvantage, even for a person quite willing to continue working; his contributions, drawn from his salary, were being withheld if he could not retire. As state employees unionized, therefore, it was hardly surprising that obligatory retirement became one of their leading goals. References to 'the sacred and acquired rights' of the functionaries became common.[10] But there was another familiar motive, inherent in unionization but by no means necessarily

conducive to the interests of the elderly: unions, white-collar perhaps
more than others, had to fight for fixed advancement and seniority
systems, and retirement was a vital ingredient of this. A public school
director, urging automatic retirement at 62, noticed that many old
teachers were ill, too tired to do their work well; but then the clincher:
'Finally, the advancement of young teachers and trainees is indefinitely
retarded.'[11]

As adopted by the state, not only to oblige the unions but also to
get rid of incompetents and more highly paid personnel (particularly
during the depression), obligatory retirement roused scattered
protest — scattered, because none of the major unions was concerned,
but very real in the context of the variety of life-styles the middle
class wished to keep open for its old age. Retirement was sometimes
brusque, with no notice, so there was little chance to organize a new
life-style.[12] Even the main functionaries' union, whose only concern
for retirees had been periodic bows to the need to raise pension levels
to match price increases, by 1939 was noting that retirement could
be a shattering experience, even if one were in good health, and
that some system of counseling might be desirable.[13]

But the most interesting evidence, as always, came from older
employees themselves. Some fought to raise the age limits of
retirement, asking of course for higher pensions in return, to the
bitter dismay of the unions. Or hear complaints by state agents listed
as 'active,' like customs officials, who were required to retire five
years earlier than the 'sedentary' group: we can often do excellent
work still at 55, and we often have considerable family expenses
too, so why must we be forced out at a set age: 'One must rest
before dying, but people who move around do not necessarily die
sooner than those who sit around.'[14] And, not surprisingly, there
was great suspicion of the youth movement behind this retirement
push. Young people often forced the old out, 'without knowing
what this means.'[15] But a postal worker, expressing the same sentiments
in the early 1930s, noted that most of the retirees managed to
continue working as auxiliaries if they wanted to. In a letter to the
Cri du Retraité (1930), he claimed that most of his colleagues
continued to work until they were too sick to do so, serving as
replacements in the same job they had held before retirement or
clerking in a private company. It was the union that forced them
into these surrogates, making it hard to talk against the 'sacred'
right of retirement even in meetings. The young were dictating
retirement to the old.

The same applied to teachers in the 1920s, many of whom worked well after 65. Small wonder that the unions, eager to protect the young, had to urge that the limits on auxiliaries be cut to age 70; apparently some middle-class people, even among employees, saw age as a period in which limited work might go on indefinitely.

In sum, employees and many managers and owners had developed definite expectations of retirement by the twentieth century, spurred by earlier pension schemes even when these had other primary purposes initially. There was at least material preparation for old age. But others in the same groups wanted variety, including flexible work opportunities, and while some were forced to abandon their interest, others proved tenacious in realizing it.

And of course the debate has continued. The middle class, increasingly an employed group, continues to prepare for old age with particular care, now in full agreement with its union representatives.[16] Their greater resources play a role here, but so does their persistent advantage in being able to plan for old age, indeed simply to realize that they will, on average, become old. Hence their private supplementary plans allow for 33 to 65 percent of earnings above the social security minimum, whereas the blue-collar plan allows but 20 percent. Moreover the new plan, again unlike the blue-collar plan, not only allows work after retirement age, while the pension is being received, but rewards this with a higher pension rate when definitive retirement occurs. And a fifth of even the 'retired' upper management personnel retain some paying job, half because they need the money, half because they simply need to work to maintain interest in life and self-expression.[17] So part of the middle-class urge to a range of choice has been maintained. And there seems little question that the recognition of the need for a range of choice, which may include work but not require it of the elderly, has spread institutionally, whereas before it stemmed more from individuals. Polls shortly after World War Two showed a pronounced revulsion against anything but mandatory retirement at age 60, on the part of the vast majority (69 percent) of the total population. But this same poll, broken down, showed the more typical middle-class view. School-teachers once retired in their majority found they aged rapidly, stopped being useful to society, and feared progressive vegetation.[18] In its inception, the slickest current periodical directed at the elderly hewed to what it thought the middle-class view was: retirement should be obligatory, indeed the retirement age lowered, and the old should get used to pleasures other than work.[19] But soon the tune changed, because the class attitude is not so simple. By 1970 the journal blasted the 'demagoguery of the young' who were not paying sufficient attention to the adequacy of pensions, though low retirement age *per se* remained a good thing. And by 1972 the whole notion of laws of retirement was termed a myth; the choice should be individual, with the possibility of retirement as early as age 60 but flexible, part-time work schemes allowing people to stay on at appropriate jobs until 70 or beyond.

This, then, was the middle-class amalgam: plan for old age, including pensions that became one's own by right; retire in many instances; but seek the ability to work, at least part-time, if one wished or needed to.

However, in stressing the complexity of this amalgam we must not bury the main point: this became the first large class a majority of whose members did, at least in a formal sense, retire. What did they expect from this act? Some claim that many have no idea at all: one group of clerks asked this question precisely and all professing the desire to retire, said, 'We'll see, but for the moment we don't know.'[20] Claims continue (but are almost impossible to prove, because of the variety of actual retirement ages) that retirees often sicken and die.[21] But against this view, the statement of French teachers, already cited, urged a surer right to retirement in 1907, to benefit from the 'repose legitimately earned to profit from some years of leisure.'[22] Not the most precise possible program, but one which indicated retirement as a state offering some possibilities for activity and interest, as against the contemporary worker view that saw retirement merely as a time, however necessary due to exhaustion, in which one would rest until death.

The middle class has not produced a decisive, unitary new life-style for old age. But by the twentieth century they were clearly moving into new areas of activity, as individual taste dictated, and this made retirement or at least reduced work loads palatable, even essential. Retirement did not, for the middle class, mean a life of total inactivity. Here, gradually and with great variety, was one of the greatest steps forward toward the modernization of old age.

Let us look again at the retirement magazines of the interwar period, including those who argued for pensions because of the exhaustion inherent in old age. These same magazines, we have already noted, served as matchmakers for older couples. Against the rather gloomy annual meeting cited earlier, teachers in Mantes, at their yearly banquet, sang and 'forgot the rules,' drinking some wine, coffee, and a bit of cognac.[23] More grandiosely and showing the effects of further modernization, if only in terms of more funds and better health, a four-day national congress of the *Fédération général des Retraités civils et militaires,* in 1960, sponsored a host of meetings, banquets, and three outings. *La Vieillesse heureuse,* as early as 1937, had a regular column on youth activities, many of which, it said, could and should be copied; travel was particularly noted, with the possibilities of specially adapted hostels in the Alps and elsewhere. Another journal tried to teach even people on low pensions how to make their own radio (and the radio remains one of the mainstays of the daily activities of the elderly in France), and this in 1929.[24] Promptings for voluntary activities, in lieu of a formal job, were of course common, for it was recognized that one might retire still full of vigor and ability. A Bordeaux pensioners' sheet reviewed and announced major sports events, including bull fights and bicycle races, urging attendance, along with offering film reviews.[25] Active participation in sports was also noted, but whether more by way of recommendation than practice is difficult to determine. More traditionally, and probably more pervasively, there was the rural retreat. Pensioners' journals published regular gardening advice. There were of course formal old age homes for the middle class. Nineteen were advertised in the Ardèche alone, in 1927, for people with pensions or with capital to turn over; for the year, 389 were listed for France as a whole, most of them quite small.[26] But far more common were advertisements for small private dwellings, passed on from one pensioner to another in many cases.[27] Small garden plots, opportunities for walks, along with fishing and hunting were often touted.[28] It was noted that small jobs, ranging from woodcutting to sales work, could also be undertaken in these places, for health and earnings alike. Many old people could have agreed with the sentiment put forward in 1857: 'I enjoy old age, because it has brought me, with the independence that is the reward of work, the experience to know how to enjoy it. . .and the leisure which lets me savor it.'[29] Here we have the basis for the new and family-independent residential pattern of the middle class traceable since the late 1930s in hosts of French villages.

Many recreational developments since World War Two have been quite humble, even for middle-class elderly, as in the proliferation of knitting clubs and other associations for human contact. Gardening fills the time of about a third of all older men. Visiting and receiving visits, reading, listening to the radio remain top leisure activities. A few changes are being suggested. There is a growing interest in travel, though this may be more verbal than real. 'Sexagenarians, septuagenarians, you have many fine days left to enjoy the charms of travel.'[30] Organized excursions have increased; white-collar retirees of the Berliet company, associating in 1952, have voyaged down the Rhone, to Bordeaux and so on in recent years. Other travel groups have ventured to Greece and elsewhere. As always, there is ambiguity here, as many still profess a fear of lack of care and strangeness, but change does seem to be occurring.

In general a growing number of retirees see their new stage of life as a time to do some new things, to develop new interests, either in leisure or work.[31] Magazines continue to keep the old up with the activities of youth, to the extent of detailed articles on how to understand the Rolling Stones, even if not on how to enjoy them.[32] Given lingering conservatism and great variety it would be ridiculous to claim a general or sudden revolution in retirement activities. But the fact is that, among the retired functionaries, the vast majority profess to have adapted well, even though they often had no precise plans on what they would do once retired. Exaggerating this trend, a leading old age magazine proclaimed, not without some truth, 'A man is no longer as old as his arteries, but only as old as his activities.'[33]

Much of this change in the situation of the elderly, from sex through new leisure and voluntary work, depends on improved health. As we have seen, with plastic surgery, sulfa drugs, and hormonal treatments many of the disadvantages of old age, as well as outright killers, have been modified or delayed, with the middle class principal beneficiaries. We can now see that the pressure brought by patients on doctors for therapy was part of a larger package, in which an active old age was seen as possible and desirable. Hence leading magazines directed at the middle-class elderly have taken to blasting a patronizing gerontology, insisting that the old be treated as active human beings who should be left alone save for specific diseases.[34]

So gradually, incompletely, one can talk about a modernization of old age in a number of aspects of life, aided by outside developments, as in medicine and the new happiness literature, but caused above all by the experiments possible to old people in the middle class, since the mid-nineteenth century, with new ways of dealing with aging as a stage of life. For middle-class wisdom, seeking control over one's destiny, and conventional fatalism were bound to clash. Old people were the last group to feel this breath of change and, more than with most other groups, their basic adaptation still continues.

However, while we can point to the evolution of new attitudes and behavior and perhaps point to these as indications of future trends, we

must not forget the hold of the past. Old age retains inherent limitations
that the new literature of exuberance may play down too strongly.
The middle class never united on a clear, single pattern of modernization;
it can easily mix new behavior with old fears. Other elements of society,
longer exposed to the conventional wisdom unadulterated, are even
slower to change. And the non-old, those who deal with the old or
younger people who are asked to think about old age, have changed
perhaps least of all. Hence for example, the 1947 poll, which revealed
that a full 54 percent of the French population, echoing the anti-
urban sentiments of nineteenth-century doctors, believed that
longevity had declined during the previous century and a half. Hence
the results reported by an observer who asked a group of teenagers to
write a description of their life at age fifty. The girls, particularly, simply
refused, giggling and embarrassed; though admitting the statistics that
showed they would live past fifty, this would put them so far past
their prime that they could not imagine what they would do.[35] While
the boys in this experiment were willing to cooperate, the evidence
cited earlier on how few functionaries have any plans for retirement,
beyond building up a pension, shows that this haziness about the reality
of old age persists. Hence the further interesting disparity: that adults
commonly believe that their parents must and should live with them,
even though they wish they could avoid this responsibility, despite the
fact that the elderly parents, successfully in most cases, operate on no
such notions of dependence.[36] Their residential goal, as we have seen,
whether urban or rural, is independence, although with frequent
contact with children and grandchildren. Greater prosperity but also
more durable marriage (less likelihood of one partner dying) and
rising remarriage rates make this feasible for most in the middle class
and even the majority of urban workers. But the traditionalism of the
'active' population in viewing the old as inherently incompetent persists,
and it goes tragically beyond parent-child relations. Hence obviously
the ease with which many institutions for the elderly continue to treat
them as vegetables, incapable of independent thought or action, an
approach which too often turns many old people into precisely the
creatures their wardens imagine them to be.[37] Hence the persistent
attitudes of both employers and unions (though modified, as we have
seen, in practice), agreeing on age 60 as a desirable retirement age.
Both groups have been deaf to rather conclusive evidence that older
workers can compensate for some reduced aptitudes by experience
and diligence, and this in a country with a rapidly aging labor force.
Here, as in other respects, the hold of customary images is outliving

any usefulness and demands rethinking, if only out of economic necessity.[38]

And the old themselves continue to be touched by the traditional culture. This indeed they can hardly avoid when so much of society around them professes it loudly. They sense, perhaps exaggerate, the hostility of the young; 76 percent of those who live with their children believe that one of the parties (usually the son- or daughter-in-law) is hostile to the arrangement: 'People don't like old folks.'[39] Their magazines, though far more forceful than before, still can plead for pity and compassion, terming old age 'the weakness of tender infancy joined with all the majesty of maturity, and with a more touching, heart-rending, even sacred character'— in other words, please give the old your love and aid.[40] Judgments of health continue to differ from facts. The old now agree that longevity has improved but they do not apply this to themselves, insisting that they will not be healthy in old age and continuing to cite the 'usury of modern life' in explaining why old age is a period of decline. Forty percent even of middle- and upper-level bureaucrats believe their health bad at 60, often, as with workers, in no relationship to the actual facts; and, as we have seen, hypochondria plus illness still reach majority proportions for the working class.

The elderly in France are not desperately unhappy. Experience often tempers the fears with which aging was anticipated, or which more commonly caused it to be ignored. The middle-class elderly, though a bit concerned about modest pensions and aspects of family relationships, profess majority contentment with their lot. And what they read, proliferating steadily for this growing group, urges them on. 'You'll remain young so long as you remain receptive and have confidence in yourself.'[41] Yet a retired engineer, healthy, living in a pleasant old age home, can still describe his life as merely a daily routine while waiting to die. And even the more active elderly interact with a society which is at best beginning to understand their outlook and potential and approve of activities — such as sex, to take an extreme — that the traditional culture condemned.

The modernization of the elderly, hacked out for the most part by the elderly themselves, is still incomplete, and its final dimensions remain unclear. The work-retirement balance, for example, has yet to be resolved, even admitting the necessity of individual variations. And the hold of tradition has still to be recognized. The attitudinal problems of aging are not products of modern life or capitalism alone. They go deeper, and hence are most firmly lodged in a society like

France that is in full contact with the traditional culture toward aging. Hopefully a new balance can be struck, as is already suggested by new behavior and new advice regarding the aging process. But unheeding custom is best broken by understanding its bases and ongoing influence, and not by pretending that aging is a recent problem against the backdrop of a more golden past. The old in France, admitting that for all their problems their situation is better than that of their parents or grandparents, already know this much. The development of modern society has unquestionably created new difficulties for the aged, in France as elsewhere. A larger historical perspective on a durable, traditional culture of aging suggests that neither recently created attitudes or institutional arrangements, even at the familial level, should draw exclusive attention in any effort to improve the situation of older people and the preparation for aging. The elderly face long-standing prejudices, which they themselves may share. As we deal with their deep historical roots we may assist in their remedy, for it is the weight of the past, not the loss of a golden age, that bears most heavily upon the aging process in modern times.

Notes

1. J.R. Tréanton, 'Les Réactions à la retraite,' *Revue Française du travail* (1958), p.149-65.
2. *Statistique de la France, Mouvement général de la population,* 1856-1951
3. *Idem,* 1861.
4. Lionel Gendron, *L'Amour après 50 ans* (Montreal, 1969), p.143.
5. Hugues Destrem, *La Vie après 50 ans* (Paris, 1966).
6. *Statistique de la France, Mouvement général de la population,* 1956-62.
7. *Cri du retraité, passim.*
8. The work-hunger of professionals, so dramatically demonstrated in retirement patterns, is more generally discussed in Peter Willmott and M. Young, *Family and Class in a London Suburb* (New York, 1960).
9. For a good survey, Joseph Flesch, *Les Régimes de retraite* (Paris, 1967). See also R. Saint-Paul and J. Audibert, *Le Nouveau régime des retraites* (Paris, 1924); Henry Lion, *Régime de retraites et prévoyance des cadres* (Paris, 1955); Robert Speyser, *L'Age du départ en retraite* (Paris, 1953); Max Horlick and A.M. Skolnik, *Private Pension Plans in West Germany and France* (Washington, 1971).
10. *L'Information des retraités de l'état,* October, 1934.
11. *Journal des retraités,* 1926.
12. *Le Cheminot retraité,* March 1938.
13. *Tribune des fonctionnaires,* 1938.
14. *L'Information du retraité du sud-ouest,* 1930.
15. *Vieillesse heureuse,* 1957.
16. See note 9.
17. 'Les Cadres retraités vus per eux-mêmes,' *Revue du travail* (1961), pp.468ff.

18. P. Paillat and A. Sauvy, 'L'Individu devant le problème de la cessation d'activité,' *Le Vieillissement de fonctions psychologiques et psycho-physiologiques* (Paris, 1961), pp. 360ff; see also Anne Marie Guillmard, *La Retraite: une morte sociale. Sociologie des conduites en situation de retraite* (Paris, 1972).
19. *Troisième Age*, 1962.
20. *Droit de Vieillir*, 1959.
21. Henri Bour and Michèle Aumont, *Le Troisième âge* (Paris, 1959).
22. E. Devinant, *La Retraite des instituteurs* (Paris, 1907).
23. *Bulletin trimestriel de l'amicale des retraités de l'enseignement de Seine-et-Oise*, 1932.
24. *Journal des retraités civils et militaires*, 1929.
25. *L'Informateur des retraités de l'état*, 1934.
26. *Le Répos des Vieux Jours, Indicateur 'Pax'*, 1927.
27. *Vieillesse heureuse*, 1939.
28. *Cri du retraité, passim.*
29. Emile Souvestre, *Souvenirs d'un vieillard* (Paris, 1857), p.22.
30. *Troisième Age*, 1965.
31. Paillat and Sauvy, 'Individu.'
32. *Troisième Age*, 1966.
33. *Troisième Age*, 1965.
34. *Troisième Age*, 1972.
35. Evelyne Sullerot, *Women, Society and Change* (New York, 1971), pp.76-7.
36. Suzanne Pacaud and M.D. Lahalle, *Attitudes, Comportements, Opinions des personnes agées dans le cadre de la famille moderne* (Paris, 1969).
37. Simone de Beauvoir, *The Coming of Age* (New York, 1972), *passim.*
38. *Troisième Age*, 1959; Alliance nationale contre la dépopulation, *Trois journées pour l'étude scientifique du vieillissement de la population*, v. 3 (Paris, 1948).
39. Pacaud and Lahalle, *Attitudes*, p.35.
40. *Nos Bons Vieux*, 1959.
41. *Vieillesse heureuse*, 1957.

7 CONCLUSION

We live in a youth culture, or so we are constantly told. Youth might deny their receipt of proper attention, but the vigor of their denials can be taken as proof of their status. The elderly, certainly, do not claim we are in a culture of the old and muster little collective vigor at all. Consider a major aspect of our societal leisure activities. We watch sports. Swimming increasingly yields its rewards to the under-20s. A Mark Spitz (remember him?) who gained Olympic glory in his mid-twenties was a wonder. He has since sold swimming suits, signed a lucrative contract to advertise milk, and failed as an actor. He's getting old. France can offer, annually, a durable 40-plus bicyclist from the Massif Central, who follows by the way the nineteenth-century canons of moderation in all things (save pedalling); he regularly completes the Tour de France though without winning, but his prowess is legitimately held to be unique for the age bracket. America has a football star, also over 40, who kicks the ball gamely and occasionally plays quarterback (which involves strenuous physical activity); this also is considered amazing. Ken Rosewall is beginning to define a comparable position in tennis. Pelé certainly approaches the same in soccer. But the point is that these people, not really old, are so exceptional. Yet in spending so much time watching the young excel in sports, and yearning with jealous amazement when someone around 40 can even stay in the game, we seem to confirm the hold of youth upon us.

Yet our spectator activities give ample room for the old. Maurice Chevalier, increasingly cited in French books on longevity, is but one case in point. He made a good thing out of being an octogenarian on the boards, and actually escaped some political trouble simply by his survival. Americans currently spend more time admiring entertainers of their parents' age and renown than any other group (some of whom also have avoided major political trouble by the majesty of survival). The youth have their own culture, but it is far from being the whole culture. The old gain more place than pessimistic assessments indicate. And many would not regard themselves as mere spectators: as gardeners who show at local displays, as pet-raisers, as *boules* players, even occasionally as marathon runners, they make their active mark.

Yet do these general remarks apply to France as a distinct cultural entity? We indicated at the outset why France was singled out for the first study in the history of aging. The reasons turned out to be wrong in large part. Most notably France did not possess a benign culture toward the elderly; quite the contrary in fact. Yet we know that France was long distinctive in the percentage of the elderly in its population and we know that France will continue to be a bellwether in this regard. Economists and some sociologists, justifying their study of the elderly, devote vast attention to the calculation of the cost effects of this growing lump of useless people in relation to the employed population. It is true that France, with its exceptional percentage of elderly and its low retirement ages, faces and will continue to face the greatest crisis in pension schemes, which in an inflationary period have to be based on current contributions by active workers but which must press these latter as the percentage of elderly steadily grows. We have seen repeated signs of distaste among younger workers for contributing to pension plans — but this was when these applied to their own remote and, to them, dubious future. Will they object similarly to increases that visibly benefit their parents? Prediction here is chancy, but the concern manifested for *one's own* elderly, initially visible in providing housing, suggests that, assuming growing prosperity, the pension burden can be accepted as successor to direct familial support. There is no indication of growing hostility to surviving parents; quite the contrary in fact, as battles over inheritance have become increasingly irrelevant. Ambiguities remain, but a modern guilt feeling seems the most striking development. France, further, has recently been overcoming aspects of traditional culture that were peculiarly hostile to the elderly. For a time distinctive in medical neglect, for example, the French have soared ahead, and, although still not research pioneers, produce an enviable average longevity record. None of this is meant to suggest a distinctively rosy future. There is still a special French history to overcome. But change there has been, and while not minimizing French distinctiveness I believe that France can be used as a measure, if not as a precise model, of the history of aging elsewhere. Just as it decisively proves that a multi-oriented culture need not be particularly neglectful of the elderly so it proves that a traditional culture can evolve.

And this suggests something of a metahistorical possibility. If one goes back to 1900, French adult longevity, geriatric conservatism in medicine and the pervasive culture toward the aged all pointed to a distinctly depressed society. We suggested at one point that possibly the pressure of the new percentage of elderly weighed France down, threatening the young and burdening the old themselves. It was the boisterous countries, even those in the throes of great social stress, who seemed most open to the idea that the old could improve their lot and expand their lifespan — most notably Germany, Russia, and the United States. The first vivification of the belief in the elderly has come with the revivification of France itself since World War Two. Perhaps triggered by the briefly rising birth rate, the existence of a younger society, it has survived this demographic aberration. Indeed it was prepared in part by the quiet, often individual efforts of the elderly even between the wars to develop a more varied life and a new image of themselves. In modern society the attitude toward the old and on the part of the old themselves, not traditional deference or a feeling of uselessness but belief in the possibility of a more vibrant style of life, may be a measure of the society itself, its own confidence and its related sense of the legitimacy of diverse choices and stages in human existence. And the elderly, even in the painful conditions of earlier industrial France, by hacking out this more diverse style of life, may be contributing to the basic *élan* of their society. They have certainly contributed, often with precious little help, to their own *élan,* and from a human standpoint this is of fundamental importance.

Much remains to be done. Individual old people play an important role in entertainment or politics, but the elderly as a group remain largely voiceless, and more so in this case in France than in the United States or Britain. There are some good reasons for this. The French pension plan, while inadequate, does not rouse great complaint among elderly interviewees, who indicate they can make do and have only modest notions of how much more they would need; the fact that their stipend is automatically tied to cost of living increases helps in this regard. The old enjoy better health than the American average, slightly better than the British, if one uses adult longevity as a crude measure (this of course conceals immense ethnic differences in America; it is in fact the healthy American old who most commonly belong to groups with some desire to exert political pressure). The rural dispersion of French older people with substantial funds and good health, their general avoidance of large 'golden age communities' in favor of individual village residence, weakens the chance for action but may also seem to make it less necessary.

Yet one must be impressed with the immense class and sex differences still prevailing in France, though not of course uniquely there. The overall history of French aging has gone from bad, to difficult, to better. Pre industrial conditions, in outlook as well as material respects, were foul, again with exceptions allowed for an occasional vigorous (and covertly resented) patriarch. With the beginnings of industrialization greater adaptive possibilities developed for one segment of the population. For the urban lower classes there seems to have been a tightening of protective family ties. Material conditions remained miserable, particularly for that majority who remained on the job. And, as indicated at the outset, historians can add aging to the list of subjects to be debated — deterioration or improvement in the industrial revolution — if they want a new version of an old game.[1] But the main point is that a break clearly occurred, beginning in the interwar period but of course emerging most clearly in the last thirty years: a break in general culture, in medicine, in the activities of old people themselves. And yet a break incomplete, because of the differentials within the elderly population.

Women's greater survival into old age is constantly studied in medicine, with inconclusive results as far as improving the situation of males is concerned. Their apparently more successful adaptation to the state, which may obviously be related, is equally interesting. It suggests, frankly, the validity of some of the traditional advice which urged the establishment of pastimes, even housework, that can be carried on into later years. It mirrors the greater diversity of interests, of identities, which women have developed in accommodation to modern society. The happiest older males seem to be those who can maintain some hold on the work ethic, which depends however on flexible job situations as offered most notably in independent professional employment, or who plump for a life of hobbies, gardening, perhaps travel and change of residence. Without question, however, though far more often studied, old men are frailer than old women; their greater dependence on a spouse for survival indicates this directly. The female model of adaptation deserves serious evaluation in this as in other stages of life.

Easier to handle, from the standpoint of conventional social history, is the class differential. The middle class first pointed the way toward a new style of life in aging. This follows from its advantageous position on the social scale — better income, better health — but also from its desire to control its lot, to defy fate where necessary. Hence a greater recognition that old age would come and an ability to plan for it materially and to some extent in outlook. Hence a belief among many that old age was not to be simply a time of passivity, if attained at all, but a time for active if calm interests. The working-class culture, traditional if heightened by aspects of the industrial experience, remains, save in individual cases, self-fulfilling. If one assumes old age as a period of vegetation, the prediction is readily borne out.

The middle-class pattern may prove neither desirable nor feasible for all; indeed, it is not uniform even within the class. Historical study suggests that debates over complete versus partial retirement (which themselves have a hoary past) have more theoretical than practical interest. The old definitely need options. Many of them, including now a new minority of the working class, have created them on their own. Fixed plans should be out. The old can produce, and indeed given their increasing numbers and health are likely to be asked to. Requirements, no; opportunities, yes.

The general culture needs constant attention from those concerned with the old (and therefore with their own later lives). From excessively pessimistic it has become excessively optimistic. This mirrors some of the hopes of the middle and upper segments of society, but it is not realistic. Eternal youth is not the answer, for it is not possible; even residents of Florida, following the Spanish quest, have found this out. There is a hucksterism about the damning gloom that pervaded literature until the last few decades that can be matched only by the shiny-bright, we'll be young until we. . .approach that has turned the published culture about. Old people in both periods have had better sense, have made more realistic adaptations, but they have been influenced by the culture available. The historical insight, among others, can do better than the facile generalizations based either on classical admonitions, unreconsidered, or on the fountain-of-youth gambit. Which is why, going beyond usual historical assessments, one concludes with suggestions for a framework of policy.

Key groups must realize the importance of tending to more than the material needs of the old. We must urge attention to the latter, but the old want more. Unions, doctors, government tend to wish the elderly away with a modest pension or a placebo. But in approaching the elderly the traditional culture must be recognized and consciously abandoned. The old look different from the young; they act differently; they are different. But they are human beings. Beyond this obvious statement, they come closer to the nineteenth-century model of old age. Healthier, not usually repulsive, yet experienced, they can offer a perspective on life that we are now missing. This is another repetition of the Ciceronian strand of nineteenth-century wisdom, but it is important. We can profit from old people, not just research them and commiserate. The proliferation of studies of pension adequacy and special housing facilities often begs the question. What do the bulk of elderly want, how can they be encouraged sensibly to want a bit more? Specific old age institutions obviously demand attention, but this will not touch the majority. If these questions are not answered, then a policy-maker is best off, judging by the French experience, setting a few material guidelines and then bowing out. For the old, as a group, seem able, increasingly, to develop their own styles of life. We may, after all, learn by listening to them.

Note

1. A final point on periodization. When statistics first became available on a nationwide basis, in 1856, people over 50 had by far the highest *per capita* suicide rate in the population (females, of course, while fitting this generalization, fell well below the male rate, indicating better adaptation and cultural conditioning, or lack of technique, or a combination). 0.008 percent of all males in the age category killed themselves annually. This was in a society marked by change — certainly not preindustrial — but predominantly agricultural and traditional still. The rate progressively declined (as that of adolescents went up) though the depression induced a brief rise. By 1962 0.002 percent of the male population over 50 (and 0.0007 percent of the female committed suicide. The same evolution held for over-60s and over-70s; once one attained 80 suicide had never been a particularly attractive way out, or at least was not so reported. More straws in the wind? Perhaps because few people were committing suicide even in 1856 (it constituted one of the lowest categories in causes of death in 1859), the phenomenon thus represents an ambiguous social measure. But the evolution may indicate that industrial society brought greater choice, greater self-esteem, in place of a social system that had relied so heavily on physical strength and property control for one's own self-evaluation. We often think of the old as having lost status. Apart from the fact that status was shaky in traditional society, the modern elderly value new options and independence highly; status is not a constant, for it rests in the eye of the beholder.

INDEX

avarice 30, 38 8
Avignon 129, 135

Beauvoir, Simone de 8, 12, 18-19, 21
Bernard, Claude 94, 108
Bicêtre, 85, 88, 97
Binet, Léon (Dr) 110-11
bladder treatment 84, 86
bleeding 91-2, 98-9, 100, 106
Bogolometz (Dr) 108, 110
Bonnamour, A. (Dr) 97
Boy-Tessier (Dr) 95, 98
brain (disease) 89-90, 92, 96-8,
    100-1
Britain 47, 85, 96, 107, 112-13,
    158
Brown Sequard 98, 108
Buffon 23, 28, 95
bureaux de bienfaisance 54, 67

Caisse nationale de retraites 52
cancer 89, 99, 101-2
Carrel, Alexis 103, 111
Charcot (Dr) 85, 87, 89, 90-1
Chateaubriand 28
Chevalier, Maurice 156
Cicero 21, 24-5, 28-9, 30, 34, 82,
    160
Colbert 58
Confédération générale du travail
    (CGT) 47-9, 50, 57, 59, 61, 63,
    68
Confédération générale du travail
    unifiée (CGTU), 48, 61

Dartigues (Dr) 109-10
demography 7, 103
Diderot 47
Durand-Fardel (Dr) 88-9, 90-2, 93-4

Eure (department) 129, 131, 133

family 56, 120, 130, 133, 135-7,
    139-40, 152-3, 157
Fédération des retraités 68
Ferran (Dr) 100
Flourons, P. 95

Galen 24, 95
Germany 45, 85, 87, 96, 105, 107,
    112-13, 121, 158
gérocomie 84
Gisors 129, 136

Goubelly, L.A. (Dr) 88

Health (and longevity) 71-2, 81-2,
    102-4, 115, 119, 122, 128,
    133-4, 153, 158
heart (disease) 87, 89, 91-2, 93-4,
    97-8, 101, 103, 105, 115
Henry IV 57
Hippocrates 24
hormones 98, 105-6, 108ff, 111
hospices 54, 67-8, 83, 102, 104,
    134
housing 125, 150
Hugo, Victor 10, 21, 24, 28

Italy, 22, 85, 104-5, 130

Josué, O. (Dr) 93 96

Lacassagne, A. *(La Verte Vieillesse)*
    23-4, 26, 33
Lafargue, Paul 50
Lamennais 24
Lecomte de Nouy 109
Léri Andre (Dr) 97
Lévy Michel (Dr) 30
liberal professions 54, 142-3
leisure 72, 74, 149ff, 159

MacArthur (General) 34
medicine 23, 29, 80-113
menopause 84, 88, 92, 99, 105-6
Metchnikoff, Elie 27, 98
Michelangelo 10, 28
Millot, J.A. (Dr) 92, 95
miners 52, 57, 61
Mono, 'Professor' 107
Montaigne 24

Niel (CGT leader) 47
Noirot, L. (Dr) 23, 25, 27

organization 35-6, 68, 70, 104,
    146-7

Paris 129-32, 135
peasantry 21-2, 43-6, 54, 127,
    130, 133-4
Péguy, Charles 24
pensions 47ff, 59ff, 130-1, 145ff
periodization 11, 132, 158-9